"Ken Posner not only takes us along as he achieves a great yet agonizingly difficult athletic accomplishment, but at the same time he displays brilliantly the beauty and history of the Hudson Valley, as well as the value of the strenuous life."

— Philip McCarthy, American 48-hour running record-setter (257 miles)

"On his solitary run, Ken takes us into the woods to meet the remarkable characters who shaped the history of the landscape. While setting a Long Path record, he nonetheless pauses to appreciate and settle us into its subtle natural wonders and profound majesty. Ken gives us a magical private tour to reveal the soul of the Catskills."

— Joan Burroughs, President, John Burroughs Association

"Here it is!—The Intelligent Man's Guide to Insanity. Why would Ken Posner, an otherwise successful financial analyst, run 350 miles from New York City to Albany over some of the roughest trails in the Hudson Valley, sleep in the wild with bears, snakes, and poison ivy, just to do it and maybe do it faster than anyone else has? Read why in this journey of natural wonders, personal discovery, and the compelling curiosity of the running temperament. P.S. He lives to tell the tale!"

— Kathrine Switzer, author of *Marathon Woman: Running the Race to Revolutionize Women's Sports* and winner of the New York City Marathon

"It's hard to imagine an outdoor adventure that starts at the George Washington Bridge. But Ken's 350-mile thru-run was exactly that, without the assistance of course markings, aid stations, a dedicated support crew, or even sometimes a navigable trail. This is an entertaining and informative read."

— Andrew Skurka, author of *The Ultimate Hiker's Gear Guide: Tools and Techniques to Hit the Trail*

"Decades of conservation work have produced a remarkable long distance trail that links together some of New York's wildest and most beautiful places. Whether you are an 'ultrathoner' or an armchair hiker (I have been both), you will find this book a captivating and lyrical journey."

— Robert Anderberg, Vice President and
General Counsel, Open Space Institute

"When you pursue your dreams, you may discover you have deep wells of strength that you never knew. And you may find yourself inspiring others to chase their dreams, too."

— Lisa Smith-Batchen, coach and motivational speaker

"Ken Posner inspires the already inspired. We are both advocates of the fastest known time (FKT). Ken Posner's FKT over the entire 350-mile Long Path highlights the importance of this historic and significant trail. His record accomplishment, despite extreme challenges, highlights the fact that Ken Posner is truly one of the most versatile, talented, and toughest distance runners of our generation!"

— Frank Giannino, two-time Transcontinental Runner
and Guinness World Records holder

"Some of us seek out unique challenges. We're looking not only to test our limits, but to forge connections with the earth and honor those who came before us. Ken follows in these footsteps, sharing his fast-paced and meaningful story in *Running the Long Path*."

— Marshall Ulrich, author of *Running on Empty:
An Ultramarathoner's Story of Love, Loss,
and a Record-Setting Run Across America*

RUNNING THE LONG PATH

RUNNING THE LONG PATH

A 350-MILE JOURNEY OF DISCOVERY IN NEW YORK'S HUDSON VALLEY

KENNETH A. POSNER

excelsior editions

AN IMPRINT OF STATE UNIVERSITY OF NEW YORK PRESS

Published by State University of New York Press, Albany

Printed in the United States of America

Excelsior Editions is an imprint of State University of New York Press

For information, contact State University of New York Press, Albany, NY
www.sunypress.edu

Production, Ryan Morris
Marketing, Kate R. Seburyamo

Library of Congress Cataloging-in-Publication Data

Names: Posner, Kenneth A., author.
Title: Running the Long Path : a 350-mile journey of discovery in New York's
  Hudson Valley / Kenneth A. Posner.
Description: Albany : State University of New York Press, [2016] | Series:
  Excelsior Editions | Includes bibliographical references and index.
Identifiers: LCCN 2016007686 (print) | LCCN 2016033651 (ebook) | ISBN
  9781438462905 (pbk : alk. paper) | ISBN 9781438462929 (e-book)
Subjects: LCSH: Posner, Kenneth A. | Long-distance runners—United States—
  Biography. | Running—New York (State)—New York.
Classification: LCC GV1061.15.P67 A3 2016 (print) | LCC GV1061.15.P67 (ebook)
  | DDC 796.42092 [B] —dc23
LC record available at https://lccn.loc.gov/2016007686

10 9 8 7 6 5 4 3 2 1

To the staff and volunteers of the
New York–New Jersey Trail Conference
for creating, blazing, and maintaining the Long Path;
to the staff of New York Road Runners Youth &
Community Services for introducing young people
to running, fitness, and a taste of the "strenuous life";
and to all the friends and family who helped me
during the run, especially my wife Sue.

Contents

Preface

This story is about an adventure in the Hudson Valley, just outside New York City. Even in our age of technology, automobiles, and concrete sprawl, there are still natural adventures out there, all around us. You just might need to look for them.

This is also a story about ultrarunning, the sport of running distances longer than a conventional marathon (26.2 miles). I'm no elite athlete. The thrill of ultrarunning is all about what ordinary people can accomplish, with a little determination, when a goal catches the imagination.

My journey along the Long Path didn't end with the last footstep, because the experience kindled in me a curiosity about the people, history, and natural world of the Hudson Valley. As I ran, walked, hiked, scrambled, stumbled, and limped down the trail, I was passing through some of the planet's most ancient forests and mountains. And I caught the echoes of some special New York voices, including Walt Whitman, John Burroughs, Thomas Cole, and Theodore Roosevelt. In these pages, I've tried to share some of what I learned along the way, together with the adventure I experienced.

Whether you run or walk, I hope you'll come to New York's Hudson Valley and give the Long Path a try. Follow the aqua blazes, and the Long Path will take you from one of the largest metropolitan areas on the planet into a secret world of astonishing natural beauty, and along the way teach you something about our heritage and maybe yourself.

—Kenneth Posner, New York City, 2016

"One more thing," he said, looking deeply into my eyes. "When I completed my pilgrimage, I painted a beautiful, immense picture that depicted everything that had happened to me here. This is the Road of the common people, and you can do the same thing, if you like. If you don't know how to paint, write something. . . ."

—Paulo Coelho, *The Pilgrimage*

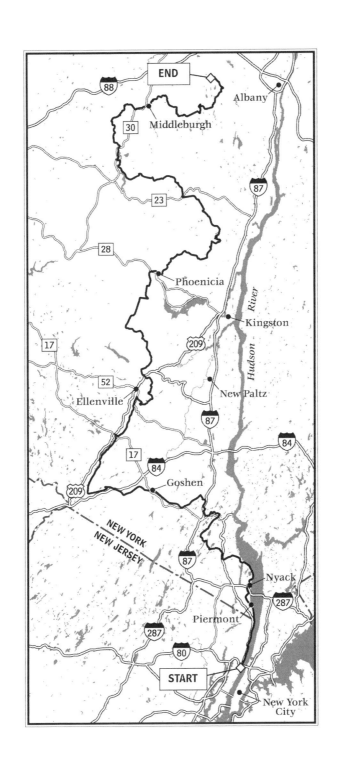

Chapter 1

A Narrow, Winding Footpath
to an Alternate Reality

Nothing in the world is worth having or worth doing unless it means effort, pain, difficulty. I have never in my life envied a human being who led an easy life. I have envied a great many people who led difficult lives and led them well.

—Theodore Roosevelt

For those not familiar with it, the Long Path is a hiking trail that runs 350 miles from the base of the George Washington Bridge in Fort Lee, New Jersey, to the John Boyd Thacher State Park some ten miles west of Albany, New York.

Inspired by Walt Whitman's poem, *Song of the Open Road*, the Long Path's creators first conceived of it as an unmarked trail that would connect New York City to the Adirondacks. Over many years, leaders and volunteers of the New York–New Jersey Trail Conference plotted its course, published information about the route, and blazed and built the trail. The Long Path was created by people who were passionate about nature, and it is maintained today by a network of volunteers for whom it is a labor of love.

Despite all the hard work of the Trail Conference and its volunteers, the Long Path is relatively unknown, especially compared to other long-distance trails. Only 119 persons had completed the full length of the Long Path when I set out to through-run it on a sunny morning in August 2013. 2012 had been a big year, with six documented completions. In 2010, there was only one.

Compare this to the granddaddy of long-distance hiking trails, the 2,180-mile Appalachian Trail, which according to the Appalachian Mountain Conservancy, a total of 14,086 persons have completed. In 2013 alone, 597 completions were reported. In other words, in a single year five times as many people completed the Appalachian Trail as had completed the Long Path in its entire lifetime—despite its being more than six times as long.

I had lived in New York for years without ever hearing of the Long Path, until one summer day when I was running on the gentle carriage trails of Minnewaska State Park with my frequent companion, Odie, the family's Labradoodle. We were passing through primeval forest shaded by hemlock, the path soft with their needles. Cresting a rise, we came upon an intersection with a narrow, winding footpath.

This path did not look promising. Rocky and overgrown, it snaked among rhododendron bushes, hopped over a muddy bank, and disappeared into shadows. A crooked sign nailed to a tree identified it as "The Long Path." But the name meant nothing to me.

As I studied this path, the wind picked up and whistled through the tree tops, and a cloud passed in front of the sun, darkening the scene. The idea of veering off onto a strange and unknown path did not seem responsible. Yet there was something intriguing about it. Odie sniffed the breeze, then looked back, waiting for direction. After careful deliberation, I decided to stick with the carriage trail, the easy and familiar choice. A moment later, the sun reemerged.

I encountered the Long Path again a few years later, this time running in Harriman State Park with my friend Todd Jennings. We came to an intersection and found a large boulder with "Times Square" stenciled in paint. I laughed out loud. As a New York City resident who knew the "real" Times Square, I thought this rock was surely some kind of joke. But no, Todd explained, this is the Long Path. It's sort of like a parallel universe, he continued, similar to our own, but where ours is big, crowded, noisy, and fast, the Long Path is small, empty, quiet, and slow. It's also a little mischievous, he added with a wink.

I snorted in derision. "One universe is enough for me," I said, elbowing him in the ribs, "let's get out of here."

∽

But as time passed, parallel universes began to seem more appealing. Working as a financial analyst at a major investment bank was exciting—but stressful. Sort of like riding on a crazy roller coaster whose rickety wooden structure you sense is going to collapse—you're just not sure when. "Small, empty, quiet, and slow" began to sound tempting.

At work, my boss suffered a heart attack. He retired on disability, and some of his responsibilities were shifted to me. Then a colleague disappeared. She was rumored to be on extended medical leave, but no one ever heard from her again, not even her closest teammates. Her workload was handed to me. I was pleased to advance in my career, yet I sensed a troubling pattern.

Then 9/11 hit. My company lost nineteen people in the World Trade Center collapse. It might have been much worse, but for the efforts of a former U.S. Army officer and decorated Vietnam veteran, Rick Rescorla, who took charge of the evacuation. Determined to do his duty to the last, he himself did not make it out.

My office was in midtown, well outside of the disaster zone. But a neighbor in my apartment building barely made it out of the World Trade Center before it came crashing down. He was one of the survivors running through the streets covered in ash.

The 9/11 attack reminded me that life is short. As much as I appreciated my job, and as proud as I was of the company where I worked, it was time to think of the bigger picture. Part of this meant getting back in shape, not only to preserve my physical health, but to keep an even mental keel in the face of volatile markets and dog-eat-dog competition.

After 9/11, I got back in the habit of going for a daily run. After a hiatus of nearly ten years, I ran my third marathon, slowly and painfully, finishing somewhere in the middle of the pack.

Up to this point, my running career had been completely undistinguished. I had taken up running in high school in an effort to improve my fitness, tired of being the last to be picked for almost every game. But as I started to run, I found that after about ten minutes, my shins would swell and go numb. The doctor explained that this was probably a condition called "chronic compartment syndrome." He stuck needles in my shin muscles to measure the pressure while I ran on a treadmill. Flummoxed by the tubes extending from my legs, I became dizzy and had to sit down. The test was interrupted, and the results were inconclusive. But that didn't stop the doctor from offering to conduct surgery that *might* alleviate the symptoms. I pictured the scalpel glinting under fluorescent lights and demurred.

Despite the condition, I persisted in running, struggling through a four-year stint in the Army and somehow surviving my first marathon. A few more years passed before I finally underwent the surgery. To my astonishment, the procedure was effective, and the problem was corrected. Now for the first time in my life, I could run freely and without pain! Determined to run another marathon and set a new personal record, I added high-intensity speed work to my training program and promptly strained the iliotibial band (ITB), a tendon on the side of the knee. ITB syndrome is a common running injury, but at the time, no one could tell me what to do about it. I threw up my hands in disgust, focused my energies on work, and put on a few pounds. Then our first child was born. The ITB healed, but running was not a priority.

Time went by, my career progressed, and I didn't do much running at all until the shock of 9/11 got me back into a daily running regime and training for the third marathon. One year later, as my fortieth birthday was starting to near, a childhood memory surfaced in my mind. I was only fifteen at the time; a friend grabbed me by the shoulder and pointed out a man who was said to have run forty miles to celebrate his fortieth birthday. We were awestruck by this feat of endurance—we had never heard of anything like it.

Now it was nearly twenty-five years later, and I found myself toying with the idea of a forty-mile birthday run. It would be an audacious goal. Perhaps it would help me take my running to the next level. I thought long and hard about the forty miles, but didn't do much about it. Soon enough my fortieth birthday came and passed, and then another birthday, and another. Even with unencumbered shins and the ITB long since healed, running such a distance was too daunting a prospect. It seemed too painful and boring.

One day during the summer of 2005, I was running along an upstate New York country lane when I fell in step with a gentleman who looked to be in his fifties. We jogged together, trading stories. Trying to impress the fellow, I said I was training for a marathon (even though I wasn't) and that I might run forty miles for my fortieth birthday (although strictly speaking, I was now forty-two). He mentioned casually that he was training for a hundred-mile race. My jaw fell. I had never heard of such a thing.

Further, I didn't think fifty-year-olds were capable of strenuous activity, let alone the unimaginable effort it would take to run one hundred miles. Working in a New York investment bank, you didn't see many fifty-year olds. Few survived in the business that long. Those who did seemed to favor golf. One fifty-year-old manager had gone to Hawaii on a hiking trip—and returned with a broken ankle—proof, I thought, that once you turned fifty, it was all downhill, and at a very steep slope. Bankers in their mid-forties complained that they were slowing down, more quickly fatigued, plagued with injuries. Get used to a larger waist size, they warned, and back off on the running—it's too hard on the knees. (Not following running as a sport at the time, I didn't know that there were elite masters who could outrace people half their age.)

I returned from this surprising encounter, still in a state of astonishment that a fifty-something could run for one hundred miles. Turning to the Internet, I googled the word "ultramarathon" and discovered that such races did indeed exist. Soon I was staring at pictures of ultrarunners traversing a sandy trail somewhere in the Marin Headlands of northern California, fascinated by their audacity and enthralled by the beauty of the coastal mountains. Something clicked. I realized that a race like this might provide the excitement, the commitment, and the goal necessary to overcome the pain and monotony of serious training.

In short order, I signed up for my first fifty-kilometer race (31.07 miles) despite great anxiety about not only the distance but the 4,500 feet of cumulative elevation gain disclosed on the event website. Why, the elevation gain was almost equivalent to a mile straight up! So concerned was I about the climbing that I sought out the steepest, tallest hill around and ran endless repeats. When race day finally arrived, it took me six hours to finish (I was tied for last place)—but the feeling of satisfaction (and relief) at having finished was intense.

I ran a couple more fifty-kilometer races, taking on steeper mountains, braving bad weather, struggling with muscle cramps and heat rash—then signed up for my first fifty-mile event, with more than a little trepidation at the prospect of nearly doubling the distance. After a good start at the fifty-miler, something disagreed with my stomach (or possibly my stomach disagreed with the idea of running fifty miles), and I became nauseous and soon could no longer eat or drink. I stumbled into the aid station at mile thirty, determined to drop out. In fact, I was just opening my mouth to ask for a ride back to the start when the volunteer looked up from the lounge chair in which he had been dozing and said, "Congratulations, you're halfway done." In the face of such encouragement, I was too embarrassed to quit. I lurched out of the aid station and staggered through the next twenty miles in a haze. When I finally reached the finish line, in second-to-last place, I was so dehydrated I couldn't talk. It took eight glasses of iced tea and a large pizza with everything on it to revive me. Then I woke up in the middle of the night, famished.

Not a particularly graceful performance. But along the way, I had achieved and then blown through my earlier goal of running forty miles on (or around) my fortieth birthday.

Over the next few years, I tackled longer distances and more difficult races. In 2008, at age forty-five, I ran my first hundred-mile race. It went surprisingly well. I immediately signed up for another hundred-miler, but this time dropped out halfway through, having failed to pace myself appropriately for a tougher course. I spent two more years training and racing, and with additional experience, my performance improved. Gradually I moved up from the back of the pack to somewhere in the middle and occasionally in the front. If I wasn't fast, at least I was getting steadier. In 2010 I completed the Badwater Ultramarathon, a 135-mile race through Death Valley, where the temperature often reaches 125 degrees. The next year I ran in the Leadville Trail 100 Run in the mountains of Colorado at elevations of up to 13,000 feet.

Why did I get hooked on these races? For one, on finally reaching the finish line, there's a thrill of accomplishment. It's like a runner's high, but the high lasts for days and weeks after the race is over. The races build self-confidence because they teach you how to manage adversity. You learn that it's okay to be tired, that you don't have to panic or get negative. You develop patience. When you're feeling good, you learn to resist getting carried away by enthusiasm. When you hit a rough patch, you troubleshoot the problem, figure out what's slowing you down, develop a plan to fix the problem or at least prevent it from getting worse—and keep moving forward. These skills help manage challenges in races and the "real" world.

"Steadfast resolution" is the most important part of character, according to one of my heroes, Theodore Roosevelt. Roosevelt was an advocate for the "strenuous life," and he credited the time he spent out West as a rancher and cowboy for giving him the strength, health, and endurance that would power an incredible array of accomplishments over the course of his life.

In his memoirs, legendary ultra-runner Scott Jurek makes a similar point: "I ran because overcoming the difficulties of an ultramarathon reminded me that I could overcome the difficulties of life, that overcoming difficulties was life."

It's not just elite athletes who feel this way. At a fifty-mile race called Rock the Ridge, which takes place on the Mohonk Preserve in upstate New York, I met a young lady who had just started running a few months earlier. When she crossed the finish line after eighteen hours, her eyes were as big as saucers, and the expression on her face shouted, "Look at what I just did!"

Writing about hundred-mile races, a free-spirited runner and author who goes under the name of Vanessa Runs explains the motivation for ultras: "It's that sense of accomplishment, self-worth, and empowerment that spills over into every other aspect of your life. It makes you hold your head up higher, gives you courage to shed those toxic relationships, inspires you in your career, helps you raise your family better, and motivates you to live healthfully and happily. That's why I run ultras, and why I encourage others to do so. The physical act of covering random mileage is indeed senseless. But knowing for a fact that your body and mind are capable of far more than you thought—that is life changing." Another wonderful aspect of ultramarathons is the beautiful locations. I've run in the coastal mountains of California, Wyoming's Grand Teton and Bighorn ranges, Death Valley, Texas hill country, the forests of Vermont, the Florida Keys, the Blue Ridge Mountains of Virginia, and the wilds of Pennsylvania.

Don't get me wrong: I have nothing against cities, office buildings, hotels, shopping malls, sidewalks, asphalt, or office cubicles. As a financial analyst, this is my world. At the same time, I've never been able to shake the feeling that the great outdoors is calling to me. It's whispering my name. Even when I'm comfortably slouched in my ergonomic desk chair, nursing the morning cappuccino, staring into the computer screen, part of me hears the wind whispering through the trees.

Apparently, I'm not the only person who feels this way. Researchers find that exposure to natural settings provides therapeutic benefits with respect to mood and health, both physical and mental (they call this "green health"), and even more when combined with exercise (they call this "green exercise"). The hypothesis is that, humans having evolved in the wild, our minds and bodies are best attuned to the natural environment and benefit from—no, *need*—an occasional break from electronics.

You can call me a "green exercise" enthusiast if you will—but I cringe at the thought of the local gym putting a potted palm next to the elliptical and selling this as a green experience. And I fear that they'll turn "green exercise" into a diet supplement, try to bottle it, or package it as something you can do in as little as six minutes a day.

There's something missing from this green movement. Green care thought-leader Richard Louv quotes Henry David Thoreau, the nineteenth-century transcendentalist and author of *Walden*, as saying, "We need the tonic of *wilderness*." Like many outdoor enthusiasts, I've read Thoreau's words closely. What Thoreau actually said was, "We need the tonic of *wildness*." And then he elaborated, "We need to witness our own limits transgressed."

∾

With time, I learned more about the Long Path. A friend ran a section along the Hudson River and posted pictures on Facebook. This time I recognized the name.

One day I discovered that a trail runner named David O'Neill had through-hiked the Long Path in 2005. The trek lasted twenty-four days. Then he came back in 2006 and ran it. This time, the journey took 12 days, 5 hours, and 17 minutes. I pondered this achievement. I considered reaching out to O'Neill and asking him about his experience, but couldn't find any contact information.

Some of my running friends had taken on multiday trail runs. If they could do it, why not I? But I hesitated. Those friends might well be stronger, fitter, younger, and more experienced than I. They might well have natural talent that I lacked.

I'm cautious, risk-averse, and a bit of an incrementalist, as befits a financial analyst. In training for my first marathon, I had followed Jeff Galloway's method, which calls for gradually extending the distance of the dreaded long run. As per his instructions, I ran twelve miles one Sunday, then came back two weeks later and ran fourteen, for a modest increase of 16.7 percent. Fast forward several weeks, and after running twenty-two miles one Sunday, two weeks later I completed twenty-four, lengthening my maximum distance by a manageable 9.1 percent. And every Sunday, those two incremental miles at the end of the long run had really hurt.

Galloway's plan was perfect for conservative people like me, for whom jumping into something unprepared seems like madness.

Now, as I contemplated the 350-mile distance of the Long Path, I thought back to the longest distance I had ever run, which was the 135-mile Badwater Ultramarathon. The step-up would be not 9.1 percent or 16.7 percent,—but rather, 259 percent. This was incomprehensible. How do you face up to a task that is so much bigger than anything you have ever done? It felt like fastening wings to your arms and leaping from a cliff.

I was intrigued. I was afraid. And now the Long Path began to whisper my name. Considering the idea was like staring at a map with a great blank spot in the middle. Uncharted territory. What would one discover on the secluded hilltops and in the secret hollows of the Hudson Valley? Imagine starting at the George Washington Bridge, the path's southern terminus, then heading north into mystery. This wouldn't be a race, it would be a journey. A pilgrimage. A crossing. An adventure.

It would be like following a yellow brick road—or sailing off into a stormy ocean after a white whale—or opening the door of a wardrobe and finding yourself in an unfamiliar forest with fauns and witches.

What made the Long Path so alluring as a challenge was that I could neither declare it feasible nor reject it as impossible. I'd wake up some mornings fired up with enthusiasm. On other days, the notion seemed a pipe-dream. Only a handful of ultrarunners tackled multiday runs of this distance. I could have reached out to them for advice, but I didn't. I couldn't think of what to ask.

This state of indecision persisted for several months. In my mind, the idea was balanced precariously, like a large glacial rock left perched on the edge of a cliff when the ice withdraws. It might stay put for centuries, or it might tip over at any moment.

I toyed with the idea, and sometimes talked with friends about it, but hadn't made any kind of commitment—until one day I found myself at Frank's Custom Shoe-Fitting, a small shoe store in Middletown, New York. If you haven't heard of Frank Giannino, all you need to know is that in 1980, he set the record for running across the entire United States, a distance of 3,100 miles, which he completed in 46 days 8 hours and 36 minutes, averaging 66.9 miles per day.

Why did he do that? Frank explains: "I am frequently asked why people do these kinds of things. I answer with one word: 'Ownership.' All of us have a burning desire to 'own' something, even if it is as simple as an endurance achievement. Once you have reached your goal, you 'own' that accomplishment, and can savor it for a lifetime. No one can ever take away from you the intrinsic satisfaction that comes from the completion of a goal. And of course, we keep on setting them." As of 2013, no one had beaten Frank's record, although the world's toughest mountaineer, adventure racer, and ultrarunner, Marshall Ulrich, gave it a good try in 2008. At age fifty-seven, Marshall completed the distance in fifty-two days, six days behind Frank, but fast enough to set the master's record (for an individual fifty years or older). It was the toughest experience of his life, he declared, well beyond climbing Mt. Everest or running through the heat of Death Valley. Marshall's philosophy is similar to Frank's: I once heard him say, "Even as you get older, don't stop setting goals."

You can find any running shoe you want on the Internet, but I made it a point to buy from Frank, hoping that some pixie dust might rub off on me. I stopped by his store one morning to pick up a pair of shoes. Frank was padding around barefoot, munching on grapes.

"You've heard about the Long Path?" I asked.

"Of course. You ought to talk to David O'Neill, he's run the whole thing," he replied.

I wanted to probe Frank, ask what he thought of that accomplishment, how he would train for the distance, or where could I find the mysterious O'Neill, when a middle-aged customer walked in, complaining that her feet hurt so much that she could barely walk the dog. Frank listened to her closely, helped her select a pair of shoes and inserts, taught her how to tie the laces more comfortably, and sent her off happy, with his personal guarantee that she could bring everything back if it didn't help. Then someone walked into the shop asking for military-style jump boots. I waited, glancing at my watch, not wanting to interrupt Frank, but growing impatient. Frank referred the paratrooper to another retailer. I was about to ask a question, when the door opened again. At this point, out of time and patience, I blurted out that I was going to run the Long Path and set a new record.

Frank smiled, raising an eyebrow ever so slightly. I bit my lip, but it was too late. I hadn't entered his store intending to make such a commitment. It had just come out. Evidently the glacial rock had tipped, and it was now rolling downhill, crashing through brush and trees.

You can't say something like that to Frank and think he'd miss it or forget. Nope, I'd as good as gone and scheduled an appointment with destiny. Not to say I couldn't postpone the appointment. My daughter talked me into running Badwater again, and that race was the focus of my training in 2012. Ashamed to face Frank, I bought my next pair of shoes over the Internet.

But when 2013 rolled around, I realized it was time to show up, step up, and deliver—or at least try. After all, about to turn fifty, I wasn't getting any younger.

Chapter 2

Stumbling Toward the Start

I tramp a perpetual journey,
My signs are a rain-proof coat and good shoes and a staff cut from
　the woods.

—Walt Whitman, *Leaves of Grass*

As 2013 got underway, it was time to train, equip, plan, and get ready. And maybe even give this challenge a shot.

But first, I needed my family's support. At dinner one evening, I brought up the topic of the Long Path and mentioned my aspiration to run it and set a new fastest-known time.

"Cool, Dad," my daughter Emeline replied, barely glancing up from her iPhone. My son, Philip, grunted inaudibly. My wife, Sue, raised an eyebrow. Odie lay quietly on the floor, eyeing the platter of chicken perched on the edge of the kitchen table.

Emeline and Philip ran on their school teams, an aptitude they inherited not from me, but from their maternal grandfather, whose best mile time in college was an impressive 4:16. I like to think that my long-distance running shows them how determination and purpose can translate into accomplishments that many wouldn't think possible. But as much as I'd enjoy it if they shared my interests, they have to follow their own paths, not mine, and it remains to be seen what kinds of adventures will capture their interest.

Sue was a competitive swimmer in college. Today she is focused on the kids. She watches them like a hawk and at the same time is their coach, confidante, and advisor, while I struggle at times to find topics of mutual interest or other ways to relate. Long-distance running is not an interest of hers, but she supports my ultrarunning endeavors, recognizing that the races help me keep an even keel. And she likes the positive attitude of ultrarunners. On occasion, when other priorities allow, she'll come along to crew or cheer.

"Maybe you'd have more fun," Sue suggested, "if you slowed down and smelled the roses."

"The best-smelling roses grow at the end of the Long Path," I replied, feeling smug to have made such a clever rejoinder.

She shrugged.

The family response wasn't particularly rousing, but I seemed to have their permission. And now it was time to shift the preparations into high gear.

To train for the Long Path, I chose three events as warm-ups and confidence builders. First, in late May, I headed up to Pittsfield, Vermont, to attempt a two-hundred-mile race. This would be the longest distance of my racing career, and it would take a lot of the anxiety out of stepping up to the Long Path's intimidating length. Each ten-mile loop started with a steep thousand-foot climb, followed by a deceptively difficult trail with lots of ups and downs. The temperature rose into the nineties, and my water ran out for several hours before I could refill. Even so, I was feeling good and moving steadily. In fact, after one hundred miles, I was in first place, a rare distinction.

Unfortunately, that first hundred miles had taken me thirty-eight hours, meaning that it was no longer mathematically possible to finish the event within the seventy-two-hour limit. I'm into tough challenges, but not impossible ones, so I withdrew from the race. On the way out, I confronted the race director, Andy Weinberg, who admitted he had made the course "so tough it was really unfair." (Indeed, none of the starters would finish.) But it was hard to be sore at Andy. For one, he's a friendly, engaging guy. But also, I respect him for his accomplishments, which include completing quintuple Ironman races. I wouldn't want him to think I was whining.

The second race was a new event, called "Manitou's Revenge." It was perfect preparation for my upcoming adventure, because the race would take place on the Long Path itself, specifically, some of the steepest, rockiest, and most difficult trails in the Catskills, including the notorious Devil's Path, which is thought by some to be one of the most dangerous hiking trails in the country. I arrived at the start on a cool June morning, excited to be running through the Catskills but not feeling particularly strong. I am rarely sick, but over the previous three weeks I had suffered in quick succession from the stomach flu, a cold, and then a hacking cough. In the process my weight had dropped five pounds, prompting a visit to the family doctor to make sure I wasn't going to waste away.

I took it easy at the start and headed out comfortably in last place. No problem, I thought, coughing ever so slightly, I'll catch back up in due course. And indeed, by mile thirty, I had passed two or three other racers. But in my weakened condition, it didn't seem prudent to spend the night on the Devil's Path. Regretfully, I withdrew.

In mid-July, I headed back north for the Vermont 100 Endurance Ride and Run, which takes place in the hills near Woodstock, just around the corner from Andy Weinberg's race. I had run this race five years earlier in 2008; in fact, it was my first hundred-mile race, and it had gone surprisingly well. Running it again would be a great way to measure the improvement after five years of serious training and racing.

It's a long drive from New York City to Woodstock, Vermont. I had planned to take off Friday from work, so as to be fresh and rested for the early Saturday morning start. But some last-minute issues required my attention, and I ended up leaving the office late Friday evening. Then I got lost on back roads and arrived only a few minutes before the 5:00 a.m. start. At this point, I had been awake for twenty-four hours straight.

The race started well enough, but it soon began to feel harder than I recalled from five years ago. By the time Sunday morning rolled along,

I had covered eighty miles or so, but had now been awake for forty hours straight and was stumbling around in the predawn darkness, nearly asleep on my feet. My finishing time was twenty-six hours, which was not only disappointing relative to my goal, but even worse, slower than my time five years earlier. Some runners thought the race had been changed to make it harder (I couldn't really tell: one back road in Vermont looks much the same as another). Perhaps I was getting slower; after all, I was five years older. Or maybe I was just tired.

The three preparatory races were not the confidence-builders I had hoped. Rather, they had yielded failure and disappointment. But now it was nearly August. If I was really going to give this challenge a try, it was time to get serious.

∾

General Dwight Eisenhower once said that, "In preparing for battle, I have always found that plans are useless, but planning is indispensable." Well, I, too, am a former U.S. Army officer, although I had reached the rank of captain, not five-star general. Twenty-seven years ago, as a young and very green officer, I had gone through U.S. Army Ranger School, and years later I still remembered many of the lessons. Eisenhower's point had been conveyed to us through the six Ps: Prior Planning Prevents Piss-Poor Performance. When it came to drafting operations orders for raids, ambushes, and patrols behind enemy lines, the Ranger Instructors had drilled into us the importance of attention to detail. If you requisitioned a radio, for example, don't forget to put down how many batteries you'd need. Was the supply sergeant supposed to read your mind?

Ranger School had taught me other lessons. How to go long periods with limited food and sleep. How to deal with being cold, wet, hungry, exhausted—and with the hallucinations, hampered cognition, and wild swings in mood that accompany extended sleep deprivation. Those experiences had prepared me for whatever challenges the Long Path might pose, or so I told myself.

I approached the Long Path through-run as if it were a military operation. For starters, I prepared a detailed route plan, which served as a basis to draw up schedules for nutrition, hydration, communications, navigation, and gear.

The initial plan was to run the Long Path in five days, averaging seventy miles per day. But as I got out to various sections of the Long Path for practice runs, I discovered that the trail was astonishingly slow. Whether it was a jaunt through Harriman State Park, or a reconnaissance to the Northern Catskills, my pace seemed to average around three miles per hour. At first, that didn't seem right, as three miles per hour is no more than a slow walk. But on reflection, I realized there were plenty of steep slopes, the kind where your heels don't even reach the ground, and the best you can do is a brisk power hike. And parts of the trail were overgrown, making it tough to see your feet and imprudent to move quickly. And many sections of the trail were covered in sharp rocks, forcing you to hop from point to point slowly and carefully.

But, still, only three miles an hour? As a three-hour marathoner, I had run 26.2 miles at a speed of 8.7 miles per hour. My best fifty-mile time was 8:34, equivalent to 5.9 miles per hour. I had finished the Leadville Hundred-Mile Trail Run in twenty-eight hours, a solid 3.5 miles per hour—and that was high in the Rockies, at altitudes where flatlanders like me gasp for breath. I couldn't fathom why my pace during even a short jaunt along the Long Path was so slow. But slow it was.

The revised plan was seven days, which would require an average of fifty miles per day. That would be roughly in line with Jennifer Pharr-Davis' record-setting pace for the Appalachian Trail. In 2011, she had completed the 2,180 mile distance in 46 days, 11 hours, and 20 minutes, averaging forty-seven miles per day (Scott Jurek subsequently beat her record by roughly three hours). Surely I could keep that pace for a single week.

Nutrition would be critical. Without enough calories, my pace would slow to a crawl. For food, I settled on freeze-dried camping meals, supplemented by dried fruit, nuts, and dark chocolate. I avoided gels, sports drinks, and energy bars, not wanting to deal with the blood sugar crash that typically follows a sugary high. The local Whole Foods store carried a wide assortment of healthy, tasty items. However, while it would be nice to have *quality* food, what was really going to matter was *quantity*.

I figured I would need about five thousand calories per day. This guess was based on an estimated expenditure of a hundred calories per mile, which I multiplied by the goal of fifty miles per day. Glancing at the list of foodstuffs, I estimated I would consume about four thousand calories per day. If these numbers were right, I'd suffer a deficit of a thousand calories per day, for a total of seven thousand over the seven days it would take to complete the Long Path.

A seven-thousand-calorie deficit didn't seem like a problem. After all, a pound of fat is supposed to contain four thousand calories. Thus the deficit was equivalent to just under two pounds of fat. Twenty-seven years ago, when I went through Ranger School, I lost fifteen pounds. I wasn't happy, but I survived. Two pounds? That seemed manageable.

I didn't want to get too precise with these calculations. I was skeptical that scientists could accurately measure calories burned during exercise. And that they really knew how many calories were contained in different foodstuffs. Their estimates were probably nothing more than educated guesswork.

This plan was good enough, I concluded, laying down pencil and pushing calculator away.

But then an image came to mind of David Horton stuffing his face with ice cream. Horton is a legendary ultrarunner and a pioneer of long-distance record-setting runs. I had watched a DVD of his 2005 run along the 2,663-mile Pacific Crest Trail, which reaches from Mexico to Canada, where he set a record of 66 days, 7 hours, and 16 minutes, averaging forty miles per day (his record has since been beaten by a day). In the video, he talked about the difficulty of getting enough calories. Ice cream was perfect, because it contained lots of calories and was easy to eat.

Dean Karnazes had made a similar point about the importance of calories during long-distance runs in his popular book, *Ultramarathon*

Man. During one of his adventures, he had ordered and eaten pizza and cheesecake while running through the night. His book includes an appendix, where he lists the calories for each food item he had consumed during this run. Karnazes was making a point: you have to replace the calories you burn.

I chewed on the pencil. Maybe a little more food would be a good idea—maybe it would be smart to build some cushion into the nutrition plan. I had intended to position six drop bags along the course, one every fifty miles or so. Well, just to be safe, I could cache a couple of extra bags. Unfortunately, as it got close to the start date, there wasn't enough time to deploy any but the original six. As a fallback, I'd pick up food from restaurants and delis along the way, I thought to myself—surely there would be many opportunities to resupply.

Next question: what to bring for bad weather? I picked up a beautiful Gore-Tex rain jacket, which weighed as much as a handful of feathers. But a few ounces here, and a few ounces there—each ounce added up to carrying more pounds than you wanted. And besides, what could happen to me in upstate New York in August? Hypothermia didn't seem like much of a risk during this time of the year. Sure enough, when I typed "hypothermia" and "August" into the web browser search bar, nothing came up. If it rained, I might get wet and uncomfortable, but it wouldn't be dangerous. (Additional research would have revealed that the Catskill Mountains, whose peaks reach four thousand feet, sport average temperatures as much as sixteen degrees lower than those in the Hudson Valley and receive fifty to seventy inches a year in precipitation, about a third more than the surrounding areas and almost enough to qualify as a rain forest.)

To document the run, and for safety, I tied a SPOT Satellite GPS Messenger to the shoulder strap of my pack. This device would track my position and broadcast the grid coordinates to family and friends, allowing them to follow my progress from afar. Rather than relying on cellphone coverage, which is spotty in upstate New York, the SPOT Messenger uses satellite telephone technology, so it ought in theory to work everywhere. By carrying the device, I would create a track of my location every few minutes, thus documenting that I had covered the entire Long Path in the time reported. As an added feature, if I got into trouble, I could press a button and send an "SOS" message, which would be routed to first responders.

The only drawback to the SPOT Messenger was that it had no display and thus provided no information to me. To see where I was, I'd need another GPS device, which would mean more weight and more batteries. And why bother? The Long Path was marked with blazes along the entire route.

But suppose I wandered off the blazed trail and couldn't find my way back? Thoreau once wrote that "A man needs only to be turned around once with his eyes shut in this world to be lost." It is only then, he continued, that "We appreciate the vastness and strangeness of nature."

Wandering around in the woods in the middle of the night, confused and disoriented—it might help me appreciate the vastness of nature, but it wouldn't help me set a new record. As a backup, I printed out detailed notes on each section of the Long Path from the Trail Conference website and stashed them in the six drop bags so I wouldn't have to carry more than a few sheets of paper at a time.

With some hesitation, I decided to bring trekking poles. As a runner, I had long regarded trekking poles with disdain, thinking them little better than walking canes. Sure, they are popular in Europe, but then again so are lederhosen. That was my attitude until I participated in Andy Weinberg's impossible two-hundred-mile race. It was late afternoon, and I was struggling up the thousand-foot climb for the fifth or sixth time that day. When finally I reached the summit, I tried to pick back up into a run, but my legs were wobbling like strands of overcooked spaghetti. At this point, a runner with trekking poles flew past, as if I were standing still. There could be only one explanation for his superior speed.

For warmth at night, I selected a "poncho liner," which is an Army-issue nylon quilt that can be tied to the inside of a plastic poncho. We had carried poncho liners in the Rangers, and I remembered curling up under one for a couple of hours sleep, then brushing off the frost and moving out on the next leg of the mission. For a sleeping mat, I considered a lightweight foam pad that weighed all of three ounces. But another three ounces here, and another three ounces there, and soon I'd be carrying fifty pounds. The mat stayed behind.

A few days before the start, I wandered into the REI store in Manhattan in search of a high-powered flashlight that I had seen advertised in a hiking magazine. The fear of stumbling around in the middle of the night searching desperately for faded blazes continued to weigh on my mind, and this light seemed potentially a sound investment. The high-powered flashlight was locked away in a cabinet, and the clerk wasn't familiar with the model, but when she found the instructions, they indicated that this light would produce up to nine hundred lumens, ten times the illumination of a typical headlamp. Fifty dollars later, it was in my possession, and I was careful to tie it down to my backpack with a length of nylon cord.

(Tying equipment down was another practice drilled into Ranger students. Everything was supposed to be tied down: canteens, rifles, radios, even hats. And not just any old way, but rather with the nylon cord tied with a bowline knot secured by an extra half-hitch and burned at the end to keep it from unraveling. One reason was to prevent loose equipment from raining down from the sky during parachute jumps. The other was to keep exhausted Rangers from losing their gear in the woods. I recalled a training mission where we were just about to reenter friendly lines after forty-eight hours of patrolling through the mountains of northern Georgia. It became apparent that a student had fallen asleep during a pause in the movement and left behind an M-60 7.62 mm machine gun, having forgotten to tie it down or having done so improperly. We had never seen the instructors so upset.)

It was time to load up the pack. I threw in a days' worth of food, a water filter, a long-sleeve T-shirt and extra pair of socks, and some other odds and ends, and then tied the poncho liner onto the back. I stared at the pack, thinking that something was missing, and after a moment

I realized I had forgotten the blister kit. I had forgotten it, because I never got blisters. But then again, I had never run 350 miles either, so into the pack it went.

Finally, I pinned on a small U.S. flag—as a salute to veterans and active-duty military personnel—and also to indicate that this wasn't just a run in the park, but rather an official quest to set a new record. In the unlikely case that a foreigner had come up with the same idea, I would be representing the United States of America.

There was more gear I could have brought along. But I didn't want to become beholden to equipment. "Men have become tools of their tools," Thoreau had written. That would not be my fate.

And why should it be? Our ancestors had covered long distances in the mountains and forests without much gear besides moccasins. As a young man, I had watched Daniel Day-Lewis in the 1992 film *Last of the Mohicans*, adapted from the immensely popular novel written by James Fenimore Cooper in 1826. I don't remember much about the film except for the opening sequence, in which Daniel Day-Lewis runs silently through the woods, carrying nothing but a musket. The imagery must have stirred something deep within me. While my family is not descended from Native Americans, nonetheless, I felt that I, too, could run silently through the woods, without carrying a lot of junk. At least I imagined so.

I stepped onto the scale. Without water, my kit weighed eight pounds. Fully loaded with a hundred ounces, it was just under fifteen.

I felt good about this. My load was light. I was ready to move far and fast.

But first, there were a few last details to take care of. If you're going after a record, you need to announce your intentions in advance. That's part of the etiquette. After all, if you suddenly appeared at the finish making claims about a new world record, but no one had known of your attempt, people might be skeptical.

I prepared a press release announcing my record-setting attempt and distributed it to a handful of reporters. The silence was deafening.

The Trail Conference took a little more interest (after all, the Long Path is their baby) and posted my announcement on their Facebook page. This post elicited some bemusement. One person complained that runners were a nuisance, almost as bad as bikers. The Long Path is a "hiking trail," the commenter explained, and asked me to stick to the roads. Others advised me to slow down and, of course, smell the roses. I bit my tongue.

Next, I sent an email around to family and friends, advising them of my plans and asking them to sponsor me by making a contribution to support free running programs for underserved youth organized by the New York Road Runners, a cause I had been supporting over the last couple of years.

I had meant to send out the email much earlier in the year, which would have given me more time to solicit contributions. But deep in my heart, there had been persistent doubts whether I would actually do this run. I had thought about sending out the email in advance of the two-hundred-mile race in Vermont back in May. But something held me back. And then the race didn't go well, and Manitou's Revenge didn't, either. Meanwhile, there was the ever-present risk that a development at work would jeopardize my training or preclude taking the necessary time off. I was never totally sure I would make it to the starting line. So I had put off the solicitation until now, only two weeks out from the planned start date.

Better late than never. I supported the free running programs organized by the New York Road Runners, thinking that it was a good idea for kids to get basic physical education, just like I did when young. Unfortunately, in recent years, many public schools have cut back on gym due to budget constraints. That's a shame. Not enough exercise, too much sugary food, it's no surprise that one-third of youngsters are overweight or obese, according to the Centers for Disease Control, which forecasts a diabetes epidemic among this generation of America's youth. Theodore Roosevelt would have been mortified.

From time to time, I would visit a school or track meet to observe New York Road Runners' programs firsthand. Once I brought along my Badwater finisher's medal and tried to explain to a group of third-graders what it meant to run 135 miles through Death Valley. A little boy took a look at my medal—and then from his backpack pulled out not one but three medals he had received from the New York Road Runners for logging his miles. I had to agree, they were just as cool as mine.

Another time, I visited a public school in Harlem and listened to a physical education teacher lecture his kids on healthy eating. Then he sent them off running laps around the gym. I recall a look of fierce determination on one little girl's face—of this Theodore Roosevelt would surely have approved.

Then I attended a free track meet organized by the New York Road Runners, where I interviewed two coaches from the Zodiacs, a running club in the south Bronx. I had noticed that the Zodiacs were winning more than their fair share of the medals.

"How do you produce such results?" I asked.

"We try to instill consistency and discipline in the kids," one of the coaches replied.

"And we make it fun," the other added. Both complimented the New York Road Runners for organizing the meet, providing free transportation, and making available training plans, incentives for the kids, and other resources.

Some of my friends agreed that getting kids fit and healthy was an important cause. Others yawned. One evening I received an email from an acquaintance, inquiring in a pointed sort of way whether I had given up my job, since I was evidently spending all my time on extreme running adventures. With sudden dismay, I realized that her company was a major shareholder in the company where I worked. Creating the wrong impression could have consequences. Brushing aside a drop of cold sweat, I carefully typed a response, explaining that no, I had not given up my job, rather, I would be using some of my vacation time for the Long Path run, while otherwise working tirelessly for the company and its shareholders. And this was all true. I checked my response carefully for typos before hitting "send." I never heard anything back.

At work, I told my boss, the CEO of our company, that I would be out on vacation in upstate New York and difficult to reach. I didn't tell him about my goal, even though he is a runner himself, having completed thirty-three marathons over the years. In our company, we applaud results—or "outcomes" as we call them. People who talk about what they're *going* to do are dismissed as "getting ready," abbreviated as "GR." If you say that someone is GR, it's not meant as a compliment. As a hedge, I forwarded the link for my SPOT Messenger to my administrative assistant. I could rely on her excellent judgment to share this information if she felt it appropriate.

And finally I tracked down the mysterious David O'Neill, thanks to my friend Todd, who it turned out had known him for many years. As a courtesy, I called David and informed him I was going to try to break his record. Then I thanked him for coming up with the idea of running the Long Path. It would not have occurred to me on my own. A gracious man, David wished me success. And he had some advice. Don't start out too fast. And beware of the distant northern sections of the Long Path, which are wild and overgrown.

Regardless of people's reactions, the word was out. There could be no backing down. It was time to stop getting ready. It was time to step up to the starting line and see what would happen.

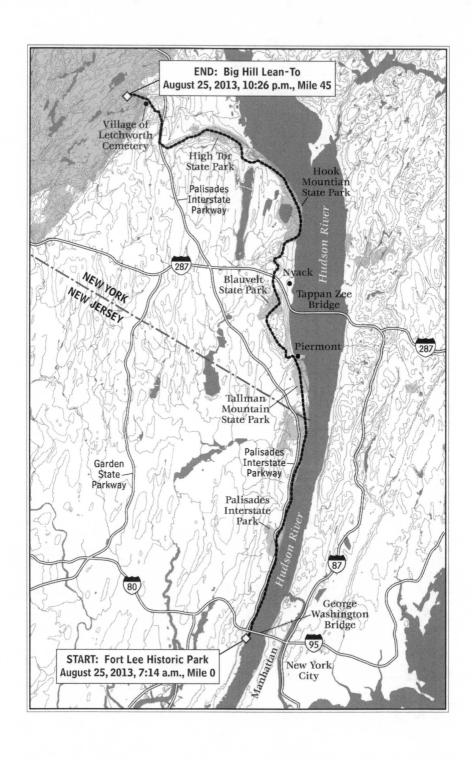

END: Big Hill Lean-To
August 25, 2013, 10:26 p.m., Mile 45

Village of
Letchworth
Cemetery

High Tor
State Park

Hook
Mountain
State Park

Palisades
Interstate
Parkway

Hudson River

287

NEW YORK

NEW JERSEY

Blauvelt
State Park

Nyack

Tappan Zee
Bridge

Piermont

287

Tallman
Mountain
State Park

Garden
State
Parkway

Palisades
Interstate
Parkway

Palisades
Interstate
Park

Hudson River

87

80

George
Washington
Bridge

95

Manhattan

New York
City

START: Fort Lee Historic Park
August 25, 2013, 7:14 a.m., Mile 0

Chapter 3

Sunshine, Gentle Breezes, and Graveyards

Afoot and light-hearted I take to the open road,
Healthy, free, the world before me,
The long brown path before me leading wherever I choose

—Walt Whitman, "Song of the Open Road"

Fort Lee Historic Park, Fort Lee, New Jersey, Sunday, August 25, 2013, 7:14 a.m.

The start was not overwhelmingly auspicious. Emeline and Philip were away at summer camp. Sue was off visiting a friend. I had spent all day Saturday in the car, driving to key points along the course to stash the resupply bags. Sunday morning, after a hearty breakfast, I hailed a cab in the neighborhood where we live in New York City. But the driver refused to negotiate a fare into New Jersey, where the Long Path starts. Instead, he deposited me unceremoniously on the New York side of the George Washington Bridge, forcing me to hoof across the span to Fort Lee, New Jersey. With that extra mile, my adventure had just expanded from 350 miles to 351. At least I was warmed up.*

---

*In 2015, the start of the Long Path was moved into New York City at the 175th Street Subway Station, which is about a quarter-mile from the George Washington Bridge, to facilitate access from across the city including airports.

Now I was standing in Fort Lee Historic Park. The sky was clear, and the morning air pleasantly cool. In addition to fully loaded camelback and trekking poles, my uniform consisted of shorts, a sleeveless T-shirt, INOV-8 brand minimalist-style trail-running shoes, and an official Trail Conference cap. The park was not yet open, and no one else was about.

I stared at a seemingly ordinary tree marked with three aqua-colored blazes, rectangular splashes of paint roughly two by three inches. A single blaze marks the trail, a double blaze signals a turn, but you see three blazes only at the terminus. A butterfly fluttered in my chest as I realized I wouldn't see three blazes again until I reached the John Boyd Thacher State Park, 350 miles away, in seven days' time, I hoped.

I took a picture of myself next to the three blazes. In the picture, my expression is confident, but you can also see a hint of perplexity. I had never undertaken a multiple-day run of anything close to this distance. My preparatory races had hardly proved I was ready. The Long Path was uncharted territory and sure to have surprises in store. To summarize: I really had no idea what I had gotten myself into. But that said, I felt healthy and free, and the trail reached out in front of me, an invitation not just to attempt a new record, but to explore and discover.

Glancing back at the three blazes one last time, I headed off at a slow trot. Aqua blazes beckoned from telephone poles, the backs of signs, concrete embankments, guardrails, rocks—anything that would take the paint and catch the hiker's eye. It felt a bit like being on an Easter egg hunt. Despite the excitement, I knew from long experience that the worst thing you can do is start out fast. My goal now was to move a little faster than walking, but not so fast as to cause fatigue or risk injury.

The blazes exited the Fort Lee Historic Park, then ducked under the on-ramp for the George Washington Bridge. Built between 1927 and 1931, the George Washington Bridge is 4,757 feet long. Its vast mass is anchored on the New York side in 280,000 tons of concrete, and on the New Jersey side it is bolted directly into the cliffs. A pulsating artery of commerce and commuting, its two decks and fourteen lanes carry 102 million vehicles per year, making it the busiest vehicular bridge in the world.

The GWB, as we New Yorkers call it, is a stunning structure, and it offers a perfect vantage point from which to admire the Manhattan skyline. On a clear fall day, you can see the city's towers with astonishing clarity, as if they were etched in steel. On a hazy summer day, you might find the bridge shrouded in fog, but that's beautiful, too, in a quiet way. When driving, you glimpse the views in quarter-second increments, which is as long as you can divert your eyes from the traffic without risking catastrophe. From the footwalk, however, you can stop and stare, drinking in the vistas to your heart's content.

Almost every weekend, Sue, Emeline, Philip, Odie, and I would travel across the GWB to escape the city for the wilds of upstate New York. Well did I know the feelings of approaching the bridge: anxiety over the prospects of tiresome delays, irritation at the tight merge off a circular on-ramp into crushing traffic, rage at the drivers who squeeze in front of you with only inches to spare. When approaching the GWB, I would always mutter to myself, "Please get me out of here," my blood pressure rising.

Automobiles get us where we seek to be, but sitting for hours in a cramped metal box exacts a toll on the human body. Studies have documented that length of commute is correlated with higher blood pressure and cholesterol, with greater risk of obesity, cardiac disease, and depression, and with shortened lifespan. I'm not surprised.

And now, what a relief to be on foot!

And what a pleasure to be on a trail, a ribbon of brown dirt, a footpath that is narrow, quiet, empty, and slow. Such a contrast with the vehicular traffic hurtling above!

A moment later, the aqua blazes emerged from underneath the bridge, crossed above a ramp, turned onto a dirt trail, and began tracing the cliffs of the New Jersey Palisades north along the Hudson River. To my amusement, the trail would one moment take me to the cliff's edge, three hundred feet above the water, and spoil me with beautiful views across the Hudson River. The next moment, the trail would sneak past a gas station or even, briefly, move out onto the shoulder of the Palisades

Parkway, cars thundering past only yards away. A little odd for a hiking trail, but the designers undoubtedly did the best they could, given the complex mixture of public and private interests that control the land. I didn't mind. It was a beautiful morning, and the sun felt pleasant on my face. Lighthearted, I was delighted to be outdoors and moving.

Even though my pace was leisurely, my attention was riveted on the next few feet of trail, to avoid tripping. Every so often, I'd glance up to make sure I had the next blaze in sight. Despite my caution, the occasional rock or root managed to trip me up. But nothing was injured save my pride, and the occasional stumbles did not affect my excitement.

An odd miniature castle built of rough stones came into view, and I paused momentarily to read a plaque on its wall. The castle memorialized the State of New Jersey Federation of Women's Clubs, which had played an important role in the preservation of the Palisades—that is, the scenic cliffs above the Hudson River along which lay the trail I was now traveling. At the turn of the century, the area was threatened by developers blasting quarries for gravel. In 1900, prodded by the Women's Clubs and other organizations, the states of New York and New Jersey came together to create the Palisades Park Commission. Theodore Roosevelt, at that time the governor of New York, explained the importance of this commission to the state legislature: "The Palisades should be preserved. They form one of the most striking and beautiful features of nature in the entire country, and their marring and ruin should be a source not merely of regret, but of shame, to our people. New Jersey is in reality less interested in their preservation than we are, although they are in her territory, for their beauty can best be observed from ours."

Roosevelt's observation was keen. Even today, New Jersey locals show less enthusiasm for the Palisades than their New York brethren across the Hudson. Recently, New Jersey municipalities granted a variance to LG Electronics to build a skyscraper that would tower above the Palisades. Under pressure from the Trail Conference and other organizations, LG Electronics ultimately decided to build a lower structure, thus preserving the view. Nonetheless, the willingness of local government to accommodate such development is a reminder to those of us who value the land that not everyone shares our priorities, and that the preservation of natural landscapes must compete against the pressure for economic improvement.

A few miles past the castle, the path brought me to a large parking lot and concession stand, where my friend Elaine Acosta was waiting. Elaine is an experienced ultrarunner, and as a member of my Badwater crew in 2012, she had helped me make it to the finish line. I had last seen her at the Vermont hundred-mile race earlier in the summer, where she finished in the top five females.

What's distinctive about Elaine is the positive energy she radiates. She's quick to smile and has a penchant for jumping exuberantly when the spirit seizes her. Pictures of her jumping at different races decorate her Facebook page, and the best photographs are taken at angles that make it look like she's flying in the sky.

"How's it going so far?" she asked.

"Fine," I replied, "except I keep tripping on my own feet."

Elaine had brought along some friends this morning. Tom, Chris, Heather, Dennis, and Matt would join me for a few miles of the journey. We continued north along the cliffs, then dropped down a staircase fashioned of large rocks, passed through the quaint riverside town of Piermont, missed a turn, caught the error, and then headed uphill and inland. Running, talking, laughing together, we were instantly a band of friends. No one asked why I was running the Long Path. No one had any questions about my journey. Rather, it was understood that running long distances through the countryside was the best possible way to spend a summer vacation. Our conversation covered a number of important topics: which were the toughest races, and who had written the best books about them; why so many people had high blood pressure, and what drugs did to help them; what foods we favored, and what kinds of shoes; and whether dogs suffered running injuries just like people.

The aqua blazes led us past several large homes perched on a steep slope. Then the trail followed a paved road to the top of a hill, where we encountered an elegant cemetery. The headstones were large, ornate, and polished. We passed soaring columns and spacious mausoleums. It felt a little over the top. Did the deceased think their fancy tombstones would impress the living? Already in good spirits, we began to giggle and then laugh out loud, lowering our voices only when we encountered a group of people paying respects.

It seemed appropriate, I thought, for the Long Path to pass by a cemetery. It was a fair reminder of where all our paths would eventually lead. Walt Whitman, poet laureate of the Long Path, had understood this point. In 1891, a group of wealthy supporters had raised several thousand dollars for Whitman to buy a house in which he might spend his remaining years in modest comfort, as he was then living in squalor—occupying a rundown house in Camden, New Jersey, with plaster falling from the ceiling. He gratefully accepted the money but spent it instead on a large granite burial house at the neighborhood cemetery. A massive, stark, elemental structure, built deep into a hillside, faced with marble, guarded by an iron gate and a bronze lock, the burial house makes quite a statement. Whitman wanted future audiences to remember him in a very special way. He had planned for his own path to continue long after he was gone.

We soon reached Nyack, the next town northward along the Hudson River. Nyack is a pretty town, with rows of brightly painted Victorian houses, neatly tended perennial gardens, and a small downtown area with cafés, bars, and restaurants. I had once stopped for lunch in this area on a beautiful spring day when the trees were in bloom, and with this memory in mind, I had set my sights on breaking here for lunch on the first day of my quest, ideally for a slice or two of pizza and a mug of beer. But I hadn't studied the map carefully enough. The Long Path crossed through a different section of town, farther uphill, and we saw only warehouses, gas stations, and fast food. I hesitated. Fast food was part of what I was hoping to leave behind on this journey. But it was getting warm in the August sun, and having already covered almost twenty miles at a steady pace, it was time to rehydrate and refuel. A quarter mile down the hill we spotted a grocery store, which seemed the best option.

I chugged a couple bottles of fruit juice and gobbled up a bowl of watermelon chunks, then faced an important decision: prepackaged spaghetti and meatballs, a sandwich, or a cup of soup? Then my eyes landed on a container of falafel balls. They looked ideal: lightweight, full of calories, all natural. I paid the cashier, sat down at a table, and bit into one. It was dry and tasteless. I could barely chew or swallow it, even with copious amounts of water to wash it down.

More calories would have been a good idea, but as they say, "time and tide wait for no man." You can't expect to set a record if you dawdle. I'd make up the calories later, I told myself, although deep down I wondered if this was the smartest decision.

I said goodbye to Elaine and her friends, picked up my gear, and headed out, feeling suddenly heavy of heart. It had been great fun to run and talk and laugh with them. The miles had passed quickly. I hadn't needed to look up from the trail, because someone was always running ahead to spot the next blaze. Now I was heading into unknown territory, alone.

After a final wave goodbye, I climbed back up the hill, turned right, and passed over Interstate 87, the "Thruway," eight lanes of traffic roaring below. Like the George Washington Bridge, the Thruway is a massive infrastructure asset, where roughly 271 million vehicles travel more than eight billion miles a year. Built in 1954 for a cost of roughly $1 billion, the Thruway reaches 426 miles from New York City to Buffalo in a more or less straight line, as it was designed to avoid hills and unnecessary curves. I looked down from the overpass at the traffic rushing below. The westbound lanes would soon skirt the southern boundary of Harriman State Park, curve to the north along Harriman's edge, and then make a beeline due north to Albany.

Follow the Thruway from New York City to Albany, and the distance is 144 miles. This is a somewhat more direct route than the Long Path, which takes 350 miles. Evidently, the Long Path's designers did not appreciate the idea that the shortest distance between two points is a straight line.

According to a recent announcement, the state of New York is working on a plan to transform the Thruway into a "Path Through History." This plan includes new signs along the highway alerting motorists to nearby historic sites, information kiosks at Thruway rest areas, and a web-based interface. According to the governor's office, the goal is to use New York's rich history to encourage tourism and local economic development. It would have been nice to put signs along the Long Path, too, but evidently there isn't enough traffic to justify the cost. The Trail Conference's website contains some information about historical sites encountered along the Long Path, but otherwise hikers or runners are left to explore paths through history on their own.

Once over the Thruway, the trail ducked behind an apartment complex. Nobody appeared to notice me as I slunk through their back yards. Did the inhabitants know they were living next to a 350-mile hiking trail? Unless they spotted the aqua blazes on the trees, it would be hard to detect the existence of a path. I felt invisible, as if I were indeed moving through a parallel universe.

The trail passed behind the apartment complex, then dropped down a slope and circled around another cemetery. This time, I didn't pause to admire the headstones. Now the trail emerged onto a sidewalk, passed a school, crossed a paved road, and hopped over the guardrail. After a short climb, the path reached the top of Hook Mountain. After scrambling the last few feet, I paused on the rocky summit to catch my breath and admire the 360-degree panorama. To the south, the Tappan Zee Bridge stood in relief above the water, and the town of Piermont lay nestled between cliffs and a large field of marsh reeds. The George Washington Bridge was now hidden behind a curve in the river, as were the buildings of Manhattan. Looking to the north, the Hudson River curled around to the left on its way toward the U.S. Military Academy at West Point. Across the river lay Westchester, while to the west I could see a lake and then the endless rolling green hills of New Jersey. It was a beautiful sunny afternoon, the sky was blue, and the views were splendid in all directions.

It was, however, a little warm. The late afternoon August sun beat down on me, and heat radiated from the black rock of the summit. I drank heavily from my camelback.

The trail continued north, undulating across a series of hills that overlooked the river, where the cliffs now reached up almost five hundred feet from the tumble of rocks along the shore. A few feet off the trail, a buck was grazing in the underbrush. He looked up as I approached. I stopped to admire the animal, a handsome young fellow with an impressive set of antlers; perhaps he was a helpful forest spirit, I thought wistfully, one who would keep watch over me in the days to come. The animal stared at me for another moment, as if evaluating this thought, then turned his head, bounded gracefully over a downed tree, and disappeared into the woods.

The hills continued for another mile; then the trail dipped into a ravine and passed yet another cemetery, the third of the day. The ridgeline gradually curved to the west, peeling away from the Hudson. At dusk, I found myself on top of High Tor. The town of Haverstraw was laid out below me under a darkening sky as if it were a toy village built for a model train set. Across the Hudson River lay the Indian Point Energy Center, its nuclear reactors no doubt humming quietly as they processed their dangerous fuel into the electrical current that would soon be powering lights across the Hudson Valley. As I descended from the peak, the sun slipped behind a range of hills, and the sky was tinged with crimson.

The view was pretty, but I had run out of water and was now licking my lips. Renowned sports scientist Tim Noakes had written a book on hydration for runners. In it he blamed the sports drink industry for selling runners on the need to drink as much water (or even better, sports drink) as they could stomach to avoid the perils of dehydration. This wasn't right, he argued. In the old days, runners didn't drink at all during marathons, and they rarely had problems. Heat sickness is correlated with effort, not with your level of hydration, as the body is capable of cooling itself through sweat even after you have lost 2 percent, 5 percent, or even 10 percent of your body weight. You'll know you are starting to get dehydrated, he wrote, when you get thirsty. So, if you're thirsty, drink, and if you're not thirsty, don't worry about it.

Heeding his advice, I hadn't bothered to drink much in the early part of the day, when the temperature was cool. In fact, at the start I had dumped out half the water in my camelback to save weight. In Nyack, I had poured a bottle of water into the camelback, partly but not fully refilling it. But it had been warm on the ridgeline, and I had sucked greedily on the hose until the last drop was gone. The only caveat to Professor Noakes's advice would be that by the time you become thirsty, you should make sure you still have something left to drink.

I recalled running out of water in the aborted two-hundred-miler in Vermont. On the backside of the mountainous loop, the trail had passed a series of fast-running mountain streams, and I had eyed each one longingly, wondering if it was safe to drink. Now in my mind I pictured the cold, clear water in those Vermont steams, pouring over slate-black rocks, and licked my lips. But there were no streams on High Tor.

Heading down the mountain in the gathering dusk, I could see lights twinkling in the distance. Might there be a deli or restaurant out there? And if so, how far would they take me off course? And supposing I went off course in search of water and didn't find any, then what?

But luck was with me, as the Long Path exited High Tor State Park onto a sidewalk that passed a gas station and convenience store. I stepped in and bought water and a beer. The beer wasn't very good; I drank half of it and threw the can away, feeling dizzy. But the water was cold and fine.

I felt a little self-conscious, sitting on the curb, pouring bottled water into a camelback with a U.S. flag pinned to the back, trekking poles leaning against a garbage can. But the store's clientele didn't seem to notice. Or if they did, they kept their opinions to themselves. They had their own Sunday evening adventures to attend to.

The water break was fortuitous. Refreshed, I was ready to push on. First, though, I pulled out the course notes and studied them. I knew the Long Path would parallel the Palisades Parkway for a mile or two, then branch off into Harriman State Park. But I had never been here before.

I stepped up to a busy intersection, pushed a button, and waited impatiently for the walk signal. Traffic whizzed by. Then the walk light clicked on.

The next step was to cross the on- and off-ramps to the Palisades Parkway. The course notes were very specific: "Be careful: Traffic moves fast here!"

Feeling like a squirrel, I scampered across, hopped over the guard-rail, and plunged into thick brush. Pushing branches aside, I searched in vain for the next blaze, swinging my expensive flashlight around, dialed up to its highest power. Nothing. Leaning on my poles, I pulled out the notes again and reread each line. There was something about a chain link fence. I looked around. No fence. It was pitch black now. Once again I panned the light around, seeing nothing but tangled brush.

Feeling a little unsure, I retraced my steps back to the on-ramp, and for good measure ran across to the far side, dodging the cars and SUVs as they accelerated to highway speed. Shining the flashlight across the ramp revealed a dull patch of aqua paint on the far guardrail, a few feet to the right of where I had jumped over. When I hopped over at this spot, the next aqua blaze was immediately visible, painted on a tree.

The path turned right, paralleled the Parkway heading north, and meandered through low-lying, swampy terrain, cars roaring by just a few yards uphill. It was slow going down here. No one but a through-hiker would venture out this way. It was just the best the designers could do, I reasoned, to link the Palisades and Harriman, part of the quirky nature of the Long Path to lurch from a mountain-top vista to a gas station, then slink through a narrow corridor between swamp and highway. The Long Path is a quintessential New York experience, I decided: seeking out beauty while navigating sprawl.

I followed the blazes carefully through this swampy wasteland. Getting lost down here was not an acceptable option. The path approached a creek, and the aqua blazes led over a stone embankment. I climbed up and crossed a narrow concrete ledge, glancing down into dark and oily water.

Eventually the path veered away from the highway and headed uphill toward Harriman State Park. There were large trees, and the footing was dry. The sounds of the highway diminished and then disappeared.

After a mile or two uphill, the trail crested the shoulder of a hill and turned downward. Taking advantage of the slope, I was trotting along steadily, when suddenly I encountered yet another cemetery, the fourth of the day. But this one wasn't particularly elegant. The glow of the light revealed a series of small T-shaped markers, planted in rows on a grassy slope. I flashed my light over the markers, but couldn't read any names.

The course notes identified this site as the Village of Letchworth Cemetery, but were otherwise silent.

Why were all the markers the same? Maybe the village had been wiped out by starvation or disease, I supposed, some kind of calamity that produced a large number of bodies all at once. Maybe the families were too poor to afford individual headstones. Maybe they didn't have a say in the matter. It was a creepy scene. The kind of place, I thought to myself, half-joking, where a hand might reach out from the clay and grasp your ankle. I breathed a sigh of relief when the path finally reached a road.

Afterwards I learned that the Village of Letchworth was an asylum for the "feeble-minded and epileptic." Built in 1911, it was initially lauded as a model institution, where the residents would live in a bucolic setting, grow their own food, and receive education and physical exercise. But over time, funding was cut, even as the population of Letchworth Village quadrupled. The staff was cut to a skeleton crew, and the institution became seriously overcrowded. The residents, largely children, lived in squalor and neglect. A TV exposé from the 1970s showed dark rooms crowded with children gibbering to themselves, sitting in strange contorted positions, half-clothed or naked, many unwashed. There were allegations of neglect and abuse, not only among the occupants, but also among the staff. The facilities were closed in 1996 and today sit vacant, in ruin.

Interred in the cemetery were 910 bodies. But the markers showed only numbers, because family members were ashamed to have relatives in an institution such as this and didn't want anyone to know their names. More recently, a state agency had erected a monument somewhere on the facility listing the names of the dead. Otherwise, Letchworth was as closed off and isolated from our normal, bustling world as if it lay in a different dimension.

∾

It was getting late. I crossed a road, headed further up into the hills, clambered up a short, steep slope, and found myself standing in front of Big Hill Lean-To. It was 10:26 p.m. According to the route plan, I was supposed to push on another ten miles. But there was no point in driving myself too hard on the first day. There was still a long ways to go.

Big Hill Lean-To was a spacious structure, with a wooden platform about ten feet wide by ten feet deep, three walls, and a roof. I sat on the edge of the lean-to and ate a freeze-dried camping meal, marveling at the distant vista of the Manhattan skyline, some thirty miles away as the crow flies, but forty-five miles along the Long Path. It had taken me a long time: fifteen hours, to be precise, an average of just 3.0 miles per hour. Well, I already knew the Long Path was slow.

I munched on my meal and stared at the Manhattan skyline, pulsating purple and orange under the misty sky. This is magic, I thought to myself. Who else tonight would be going to sleep with a view of the New York City skyline just outside their bedroom?

The first day had gone well. I had covered a lot of ground, taken in magnificent vistas, run with friends in good cheer, and felt the August sunshine and summer breeze on my cheek. I had followed a soft trail under quiet trees and over rolling hills and encountered a young buck, possibly a forest spirit who would keep an eye on me in the days to come. I had food and water and shelter. I felt strong and happy to be alive.

Forty-five miles down, three hundred and five to go. The remaining distance, while slightly reduced from the total, remained incomprehensible, more than double anything I had ever done.

One day down, and six left—if I stayed on schedule. I was, however, already ten miles behind plan.

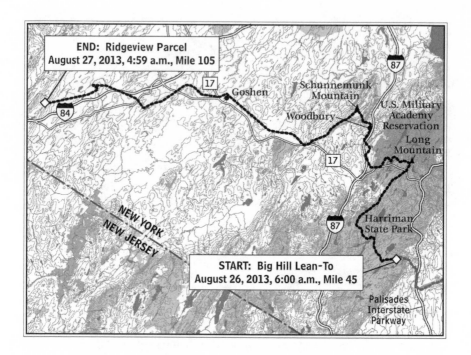

END: Ridgeview Parcel
August 27, 2013, 4:59 a.m., Mile 105

Goshen

Schunnemunk
Mountain

Woodbury

U.S. Military
Academy
Reservation

Long
Mountain

NEW YORK
NEW JERSEY

Harriman
State Park

START: Big Hill Lean-To
August 26, 2013, 6:00 a.m., Mile 45

Palisades
Interstate
Parkway

Chapter 4

The First Storm

He traveling with me needs the best blood, thews, endurance,
None may come to the trial till he or she bring courage and health,
Come not here if you have already spent the best of yourself,
Only those may come who come in sweet and determin'd bodies

—Walt Whitman, "Song of the Open Road"

Big Hill Lean-To, Harriman State Park,
Monday, August 26, 2013, 6:00 a.m.

I woke up at the crack of dawn, feeling excited and energetic—and this even without my usual morning cappuccino. However, I immediately faced two challenges.

First, there was no breakfast. Apparently my pack contained only a single meal, which I had devoured the night before while admiring the Manhattan skyline. Under the logistics plan, a second meal should have been packed for breakfast. Well, this oversight wouldn't be fatal. The first drop bag was waiting for me about fifteen miles down the trail. In the meantime, a handful of dried fruit and nuts would have to serve. I'd make up for the growing calorie deficit a little later.

Second, the overnight plan wasn't completely hashed out. The next lean-to was over one hundred miles in the distance. Surely there'd be a comfortable stretch of trail to rest in place somewhere along the way—as long as it didn't rain. In the unlikely event of rain, I'd keep moving.

Having formulated this plan and munched on a handful of dried apricots, it was time to get going.

As I headed out, I tried not to worry too much about what the day would hold. Instead, I focused on the here and now. Trotting down the hill from the lean-to, I felt strong and upbeat, happy to be in motion again, excited to be starting out on day two of this adventure.

The Long Path joined an old logging road, wide and grassy and sloping slightly downhill. This was a perfect place to pick up speed and make up time, and I fell into a steady rhythm. A few minutes went by before I remembered to look up—and to my consternation, the blazes were gone. Slowing to a walk, I scoured the edge of the woods for aqua clues. The logging road terminated at a paved road. This was not right. Backtracking a couple of hundred yards, I found the turn-off. Somewhat chastened, I moved out again, this time at a more measured pace, careful to look up every few steps.

Following blazes when you're running is not as simple as it sounds. Runners move faster than hikers, so the blazes go by quickly. And runners need to look *down* at their feet, to avoid tripping—especially when the trail is rough, as hiking trails in the northeastern United States typically are. Look down too much, and you miss the blaze and get lost. Look up too much and you stumble and fall on sharp rocks. Neither outcome is good, especially if you're trying to set a record.

In any case, I was now trying to run through (without stumbling) Harriman State Park, the second-largest park in New York after the Adirondacks. Harriman consists of 46,000 acres and includes 225 miles of hiking trails, which are maintained by the New York–New Jersey Trail Conference and its cohorts of volunteers. The park was created in 1910 when Mary Averell Harriman, widow of railroad tycoon E. H. Harriman, contributed ten thousand acres from the estate and a check for $1 million to the State of New Jersey in a deal to not only create a major park but block construction of a prison at nearby Bear Mountain, which was evidently not considered an amenity for the neighborhood. The land was handed over to the Palisades Interstate Park Commission, the same body that Theodore Roosevelt and the governor of New Jersey had created in 1900 to preserve the cliffs above the Hudson River.

In 1929, Harriman's son, Averell, who was later to become governor of New York, commemorated the formation of Harriman State Park by commissioning a statue of Walt Whitman, which was eventually located at Bear Mountain, only a few miles away from my current location. Stanzas from Whitman's "Song of the Open Road" were carved into a nearby granite ledge.

Today regarded as the "poet of democracy," Whitman was controversial during his lifetime. His poetry affirms opportunity, movement, restlessness, sexual energy, radical self-consciousness, and destruction of rules, characteristic of America's emerging sense of self-identity in the late nineteenth century. But it violated the conventional norms of those times. It ignored ornamentation, literary allusion, romance, rhyme, anything that existed for the sake of tradition alone. And some parts were thought to be obscene. In fact, the city of Boston threatened legal action against his publisher.

"I know I am restless and I make others so," he wrote, "for I confront peace, security, and all the settled laws, to unsettle them."

It's a little ironic to find Whitman ensconced as the patron saint of hikers. Whitman was more a man of the cities and the people than the wilderness. He spent his life in Brooklyn, Manhattan, Washington, D.C., and Camden, New Jersey. He particularly loved Manhattan, which he regarded as a "proud and passionate city—mettlesome, mad, extravagant city." "Manhattan! How fit a name for America's great democratic island city! The word itself, how beautiful! How aboriginal! How it seems to rise with tall spires, glistening in sunshine, with such New World atmosphere, vista and action!"

Further, while Whitman would go for walks, he would not have considered himself a hiker. Rather, he styled himself a "loafer." His famous *Song of Myself* begins "I lean and loafe at my ease observing a spear of summer grass."

The term "loafer" referred to a city rough, someone who gambled, drank, and cursed. As a young man, Whitman was once fired from a job for "indolence." On the inside cover of his book of poems, the portrait shows him in cheap clothes, shirt open at the neck, one hand on his hip, hat pitched rakishly back on his head.

The "long brown path" from the first stanza of "Song of the Open Road" was a metaphor for the sense of opportunity that Americans felt at the turn of the century, individually and as a nation of growing strength, prosperity, and importance on the world stage. In telling people to seek the long brown path, Whitman was encouraging them to look forward and embrace their path through life, whatever it might be. He wasn't suggesting a hike in the woods. What would he have thought of a 350-mile run through the wilderness? That would be anybody's guess.

From the air, Harriman stands out as a large forested plateau with rippling mountain ridges and lakes, a break between the wide open space of the Wallkill Valley to the north and the plains of New Jersey to the south. Harriman's mountains are ancient. There are granite rock outcroppings in the park that are over a billion years old, remnants of the original tectonic plate from which ancestral North America was born. These rocks have endured countless climatic cycles. As recently as twenty thousand years ago, the region was covered by a continental ice sheet thousands of feet thick, which stretched all the way down from northern Canada. Glaciers carved out U-shaped valleys, scraped over and smoothed the ridgelines, and as they receded left behind thirty-two lakes, countless ponds and bogs, and endless jumbles of rock.

While it's a popular park, Harriman creates an impression of solitude. The traveler meanders through series of small valleys, each a separate compartment, quiet, shaded, and isolated by a low ridgeline from its neighbors. In one area, the Long Path passes between steep valley walls and a marsh fringed with cattails. A moment later, the path surmounts a modest hillock covered in wavy grass. The soil contains much debris left behind by the glaciers, and the trail is often rocky.

Passing through Times Square, I smiled at the stenciled white paint on the gray rock. I used to work in an office building right in the middle of the "real" Times Square, the one located in Manhattan, where the thick crowds make it hard to walk down the sidewalk during the day, and where on News Year's Eve, the mob swells to an estimated two million people. This morning the parallel universe was indeed empty and quiet. No one else was here. I didn't encounter another soul over the next ten miles.

A few hours later, the path reached Route 6, a two-lane highway that bisects the northern reaches of Harriman, connecting the Palisades Parkway with the Thruway. Standing by the guardrail, I watched the cars zipping past before picking a break in the traffic to scurry across the road and into a parking lot.

On the edge of the lot stood a kiosk welcoming visitors to Long Mountain and the Long Path. The sign admonished:

> Take nothing but pictures.
> Leave nothing but footprints.
> Kill nothing but time.

I hiked in counting my steps, turned right into a field of blueberry bushes, and reached behind a log. Yes! There was my first drop bag, exactly where I had stashed it two days ago. The contents of a large water bottle went straight into the camelback's bladder. Two freeze-dried meals, more dried fruit and nuts, and another chocolate bar went into the pack. I emptied my accumulated trash into a garbage bag, zipped up the drop bag, and carefully repositioned it behind the log—all the while looking around me with a guilty expression. After all, I wasn't supposed to leave anything but footprints.

(One evening a few weeks later, I returned to the parking lot off Route 6. I counted my paces along the path in the darkness, waded through the bushes, reached behind a log and yes! retrieved the drop bag. I didn't leave any trash behind, and probably not even a footprint.)

Back on the trail, I encountered the first people I'd seen all day, a mom and two kids, and fell in behind them on the short hike to the summit of Long Mountain. At the top, we admired a plaque carved into the granite in memory of Raymond Torrey, one of the founders of the New York–New Jersey Trail Conference and an early champion of the Long Path.

He had been quite a character, I learned afterward. Torrey was widely known for his popular weekly column in the *New York Evening Post*, which he called "The Long Brown Path" in a nod to Whitman's poem. In this column, Torrey shared news from regional hiking clubs, described popular trails, and championed environmental causes. He was himself an avid hiker and trailblazer, and he spearheaded volunteer efforts to build a network of trails throughout Harriman State Park. In 1921, he became an advocate of the Appalachian Trail, and over the next ten years was instrumental in routing, blazing, and clearing over 160 miles of the trail from New Jersey to Connecticut.

The idea for the Long Path was attributed to Paul and Vincent Schaefer of the Mohawk Valley Hiking Club, who had come up with the idea for a long-distance hiking trail, similar in spirit to the Long Trail in Vermont, the Pacific Coast Trail and John Muir Trails out west, and of course the Appalachian Trail, but in this case linking New York City and the Adirondacks. From March through June 1934, Torrey devoted his popular column to describing the proposed route for the Long Path.

But Torrey wasn't just a trailblazer. Interested in botany since childhood, he was an amateur naturalist and extremely well versed in the flora and fauna of the Hudson Valley. In fact, he could reputedly identify seven hundred different plants, was especially interested in boreal species found at high elevations, and became an authority on lichens.

In a bid to gain allies, master planner, builder, and New York power broker Robert Moses had appointed Torrey to the New York State Parks Council. But in 1929, the two men disagreed on the proposed routing of a parkway across Long Island. When Moses learned that Torrey had published information about the proposed parkway to rally opposition, he summoned Torrey to his office and berated him. Torrey defended himself. The argument escalated until Moses flew into a rage, his face alternately paling and purpling. "God damn you!" he shouted. Torrey responded with an insult. Lunging from his chair, Moses seized Torrey by the throat and began choking him. Other council members pulled him off and ushered Torrey out of the room, but as they were leaving, Moses broke free, picked up a heavy smoking stand with a three-foot steel base, and shouting "You goddamned son of a bitch," hurled the heavy missile after him. Fortunately it missed.

Moses was master of the long *gray* path: he built countless roadways and other projects throughout the New York City metropolitan area. Indeed, he was instrumental in developing the Palisades Parkway, along whose swampy shoulder I had trudged the night before. His reputation was marred, however, by his disdain for the public and the heavy-handed manner in which he forced through big projects, for example the Cross Bronx Expressway, where he evicted thousands of people without compensation. Moses was brilliant, but his pugnacious style created enemies, and he was eventually forced from power. As an old man, he wondered aloud why great men were not shown more gratitude.

Torrey passed away in 1938 from a heart attack, and friends scattered his ashes on Long Mountain, his favorite viewpoint in the Hudson Valley. And here I was, seventy-five years later, standing on the same spot.

I had crossed Long Mountain in late July on a training run and had glanced at the plaque, but hadn't bothered to read it, assuming it would laud him as an organizer, conservationist, and champion of the Long Path.

Nor did I read it this time. After all, the clock was ticking.

I didn't read the words until later that fall, after my through-run was over, when on a cloudy afternoon I returned to Long Mountain with Sue, my son Philip, and Odie. We made the short hike to the summit and paused to admire the view south to Bear Mountain and north to Turkey Pond. The sky was gray, but I recall a stand of beeches with bright yellow leaves. This time I read the words on the plaque, and to my surprise found that Raymond Torrey was described as "A Great Disciple of the Long Brown Path."

"Disciple" means "follower or student." He must have conveyed a sense of humility to be remembered this way. For there is no questioning the vigor with which he pursued his own path through life or the magnitude of his contributions to land preservation, trail stewardship, and the hiking and outdoors community.

∽

The mom and her kids turned back to the parking lot, while I kept going. Drops of rain began to spatter across the granite summit. I scooted downhill, seeking shelter under trees. Clambering down a steep embankment, I found myself in a U-shaped valley, carved by an ancient glacier, with a stream snaking across the valley floor. Suddenly a small frog jumped out from under my feet. Then another did the same. It soon became apparent that the valley floor was covered with small frogs. With each step, another frog leaped for cover, usually into a nearby puddle, uttering a squeak of alarm and making a tiny splash. I stepped carefully.

After crossing the stream, I struggled up a steep slope on the far side of the valley until the path reached a grassy ridgeline, after which it dropped back down into another valley. According to the Trail Conference notes, the path was now skirting the boundary of the U.S. Military Academy reservation. The trail became damp and overgrown, and the going was slow. A solitary cardinal flower grew next to the path, its brilliant red petals flashing from a tall stalk. It was pretty, but I wasn't here to smell the flowers. The trail wound its way back uphill again. The slow pace was frustrating.

Eventually the trail emerged on the top of the ridgeline and then, to my surprise, skirted the shoulder of Route 6, only a few yards away from the traffic. Cars went rushing by westbound to the Thruway and eastbound to the Palisades Parkway. Now on top of the mountain, I felt vindicated for having persevered through the slow, overgrown, uphill sections. It would now be all downhill from here, at least until the next mountain. Glancing at the heavy traffic, I once again felt grateful to be on foot.

The reunion with Route 6 lasted only a few yards. The trail soon veered to the right through a grassy field and dropped down the hillside onto an abandoned road. The pavement was a welcome break from the trail, although this road had seen better days. Grass grew through cracks in the asphalt, tangled brush encroached on the shoulders, trees leaned over the shoulder. It seemed a little sad to find a roadway that had fallen into such disrepair. Abandoned roads, ruins, cemeteries, memorials— with each step, the Long Path seemed to be taking me further back in time. This old road was just another lesson in decay.

Then I had a strange, apocalyptic vision: perhaps this abandoned road would lead through a ruined metropolis and into a desert wasteland, where I would stumble upon the Statue of Liberty overturned and half-buried in the sand.

But this did not happen. Instead, in a mile or so the path turned onto an active road, whose slick asphalt led downhill and through the outskirts of the town of Woodbury, which is known for its enormous outlet mall. I recalled a family visit to the mall a few years ago, how it had taken so much time to fight our way in, find a spot, and park the car; how I had shut off the engine and looked around in dismay at an ocean of stationary vehicles. To be fair, we did fully outfit Philip for his freshmen year of high school at rock-bottom prices. Even so, it had seemed an outrage against nature to spend such a beautiful day driving and shopping.

Fortunately, the Long Path was not going anywhere near the mall. Unfortunately, I was once again out of water and just beginning to fantasize about cold beers and burbling mountain brooks when suddenly a golf course came into view. Taking a chance, I sauntered over to the clubhouse, swung open the door, and stepped into the lobby. I found myself standing on a polished marble floor, eying a crystal chandelier above and peering into an empty restaurant decorated in dark wood paneling. Dressed in a sleeveless shirt and muddy shoes, I surely fit right in.

A manager emerged from an interior office and squinted at me, trying to process the strange image of a spectral figure emerging from a parallel universe where people hike or run for hundreds of miles. I tried to explain my mission. He didn't seem to understand much of what I was saying, except the part about needing water. After glancing at the restaurant, and then thinking better of it, he pointed me to the restroom. I refilled my camelback from a gold-plated faucet.

On the way out, I waved thank you, but he was deeply engrossed, reviewing a computer printout with two assistants. They didn't see me. The parallel universe had swallowed me back up again.

And now as the Long Path curved westward into the Wallkill Valley, it was once again time to cross the Thruway and its eight lanes of thundering traffic headed north to Albany and south to New York City. I trotted through an underpass, the roar above strangely muffled.

I dislike highways. It's a struggle to keep my temper in heavy traffic. I get mad at people who drive slowly in the left lane or whip by speedily in the right. Maybe I'm just not patient enough. I don't like waiting for stoplights, especially if they're poorly synchronized and I hit two reds in a row. I fume when the elevator is slow to arrive. After a nice meal at a pleasant restaurant, I start scanning the room for the waiter, ready to sign the check and leave. If the waiter's slow to appear, I've been known to stand up, credit card in hand, and go looking for them. (My wife Sue finds this behavior extremely mortifying.)

The problem with highways is that they require compromise. Along the Thruway's wide and straight lanes a solitary individual could race at a hundred miles per hour. But as great crowds of people use the highway all at once, the law limits us to sixty-five—even if the road is empty. And then, when traffic gets congested, we slow even further. Someone taps the brakes, and the disturbance percolates in the form of a compression wave: traffic slows, then reaccelerates, then slows again, with no visible cause. Not to mention the nightmare that results when there's an accident. Sure, the system moves multitudes of people along great distances at the lowest possible cost. No question, it's the greatest good for the largest number of people. But the individual cannot exercise his or her capabilities at their limit. On the Long Path, however, these obstacles do not present themselves. You can go as fast as you want. You don't have to wait for a soul.

Once through the underpass, the blazes turned onto a dirt road alongside a gas-line right of way. On the left lay a swamp. On the right was a railroad line. For the first time on this journey, I began to feel weary. The road seemed to go on much farther than the mileage indicated in the notes. I became convinced that the Trail Conference had systematically underestimated the distances—a perfect explanation for why my pace on the Long Path was so absurdly slow. I vowed to set them straight on this once my quest was over.

After an interminable distance, the dirt road came to an end; the trail crossed underneath an ancient railway trestle, then looped right back up to the Thruway, paralleling the shoulder of the highway for a final two hundred yards—as if the Long Path were reluctant to bid adieu to those eight lanes of thundering asphalt (an absurd image comes to mind, of a Chihuahua dogging the heels of a Great Dane). I drank in the sounds and smells of the traffic, hopefully for the last time. Then the trail looped back down, crossed a creek and then a road, and worked its way along an active railroad line. To my tired mind, each zig of this circuitous route seemed far longer than the distance listed in the notes, and so did the zags.

It had somehow become midafternoon. From the railroad line, the path was now working its way up Schunemunk Mountain, a long ridge that marks the eastern edge of the Great Appalachian Valley. I had never been here before, but my friend Todd Jennings had told me it was his favorite trail in the Hudson Valley and a magical place.

The trail became steep, and I clambered up a succession of rocky ledges, fancying myself a sailor climbing up the rigging toward a crow's nest high on the mast. But rather than grasping ropes, I was grabbing handholds of a crumbly grayish-purple sandstone full of large pebbles and speckled with green lichen. According to the Trail Conference notes, this rock is called Schunemunk puddingstone. It's a sedimentary matrix containing fragments of quartz, quartzite, and shale, laid down some three hundred to four hundred million years ago.

Reaching Schunemunk's 1,664-foot summit, I paused and looked about. The Thruway was clearly visible far below, making its way up from the south. Across the way stood the mountain ridges of Harriman, and behind them, the wide plains of the Wallkill Valley opening to the west, where I would soon be headed. To the north, the Thruway disappeared into distant haze. The Catskill Mountains were visible as a blur along the horizon. Hopefully I would be somewhere out there in a few days. Overhead, the sky was murky, with tendrils of mist snaking through the atmosphere.

In 1777, Schunemunk Mountain witnessed a brief firefight. Lieutenant Jacob Roosa had recruited a band of Rangers from poor tenant farmers in the Catskills with the promise of generous land grants. Their mission was to link up with British forces in New York City. "Rose's Rangers," as they came to be known, made their way south from the Catskills, and after camping out in the Shawangunk Mountains, were attempting to infiltrate through the Wallkill Valley when they encountered American revolutionary forces.

"Rangers" were the unconventional forces of the eighteenth century. Consisting of frontiersman, Indians, and freed slaves, Rangers were skilled woodsmen capable of covering long distances on foot and fighting in small groups. As a young U.S. Army Ranger student in the late twentieth century, I had been required to memorize the standing orders for Roger's Rangers, who had fought further north in the Adirondack Mountains of upstate New York during the French and Indian Wars. I still remembered order number one: "Don't forget nothing."

Lieutenant Roosa may or may not have forgotten anything, but he was unable to keep his movements concealed. American forces ambushed his band at the base of Schunemunk Mountain, killing five and taking the rest prisoner. Most of Rose's Rangers were eventually freed, but Lieutenant Roosa was hanged for treason.

Schunemunk Mountain has two peaks separated by a swampy area in a rocky cleft, and it took a long time to cross the ridge. Eventually a radio tower came into sight and marked the beginning of the descent. Feeling a little tired, I was shuffling along slowly, when a strange figure materialized in front of me. It was Todd!

"How're you doing?" he asked.

"I'm doing great," I replied, and all of a sudden I did feel great, because it made such a difference to have company again. As we trotted along, Todd kept me entertained with stories about the towns, farmland, countryside, and history of the area we were passing through. We continued together for a few miles until Todd broke off to retrieve his car, promising to meet me again in the town of Goshen some fifteen miles down the trail for pizza and beer.

After descending from Schunemunk, the path followed an overpass over Route 17, a four-lane highway that leads from the Thruway westward through the Wallkill Valley, skirting the southwestern boundary of the Catskills. After crossing the highway, the Long Path turned onto the Heritage Valley Rail Trail and then immediately passed back underneath Route 17 and paralleled the highway heading west. Joggers and cyclists were passing to and fro on the rail trail, which was smoothly paved.

It was dusk, probably just after 7:00 p.m., and I was determined to make it to Goshen before 10:00 p.m., which was closing time at Kelly Jean's, the restaurant where I had cached the next drop bag and where I planned to meet Todd for pizza and beer. Ten miles would be three hours at a walking pace, but only two and a half at a slow jog. Getting there late was not an option: not only would I miss out on a meal, but I might not be able to retrieve the drop bag—which would be a disaster. I picked up my feet and moved out, tapping the trail with my trekking poles, trying to remember what it felt like to run on a smooth surface. My feet found some sort of rhythm, and I made steady progress.

To the north were wide fields. This area is known for its fertile black earth, which produces robust crops of onion and celery. Roughly eighteen thousand years ago, the Wallkill Valley was filled with a wide lake, created as the runoff from melting ice pooled against the moraines and other debris left behind by retreating glaciers. The stagnant water was evidently covered with a mat of vegetation, and on the bottom of the lake fine-grained, rich organic sediment accumulated, forming deep beds of black muck. Thousands of years later, when frontiersmen drained the land, the black muck would yield fertile soil for farming. The black muck also yielded the bones of prehistoric mammals that frequented the glacial lake, including mastodons, distant relatives of modern elephants. In 1801, a mastodon skeleton from this area became the first full prehistoric skeleton to be put on public display. It must have created a sensation.

Twilight fell, and the sky darkened. After a while, it began to drizzle. I scooted to the edge of the trail for some shelter under the trees. It rained harder. There was a blinding flash to the south. I counted to five and then thunder crashed. Now the rain began to pour. I was quickly soaked. It took another half hour to reach Goshen. As I splashed through the town square, rain running down my face, I lost the blazes, came to a stop in the middle of the street, and shined my flashlight on full power all around me. A police cruiser sat parked down the block, but the officers apparently didn't think I looked suspicious, or perhaps they weren't paying attention. I finally made it to Kelly Jeans around 9:30 p.m.

Todd was waiting for me. He had thoughtfully brought a towel. I retreated to the washroom, where I discretely wrung out my wet clothing in the sink and tried to dry off.

Our waitress took good care of us, bringing plenty of food and beer, and then as I was longing for the Gore-Tex jacket (which had been left behind because it weighed more than a feather), she rustled up a large garbage bag, which I fashioned into a field-expedient poncho. Kelly Jean, the proprietress of the establishment, stopped by to wish me luck, and a couple of the patrons at the bar raised their glasses in a toast. My spirits were considerably lifted. After an hour's break, it was time to head out into the rain again.

My spirits remained lifted for the next four miles, after which the steady rain wore them down. The garbage bag did a good job shielding me from the precipitation, but it prevented my sweat from dissipating, and soon I was thoroughly damp. Even worse, it had been treated to repel rodents, and it stank to high heaven. The treatment must have worked. As long as I wore the noxious plastic, the local rodents kept their distance—I never heard so much as a squeak.

Leaving Goshen, the path turned right at a cemetery (number five so far), and then crossed underneath Route 17 one more time. After a few miles on a grassy trail, the path moved back onto roads and passed a few ramshackle buildings. The rain intensified. I took shelter for a few minutes under the overhang of a deserted apartment building.

When a young Theodore Roosevelt went buffalo hunting in Montana for the first time, he was met with a steady cold rain. Awakening in the middle of night to find himself lying in four inches of water, he was nevertheless heard to exclaim, "By Godfrey, but this is fun!" Well, right now, I wasn't measuring up to his standard.

The rain slacked off, and I headed out again to tackle fourteen endless miles of pavement before the Long Path would return to the woods. An hour went by, and my feet began to hurt. This was a surprise, as I had plenty of experience with wet feet, and rarely had problems. Regardless, when something hurts, it's best to troubleshoot. I pulled over at an abandoned gas station next to an abandoned railway track. A line of old freight cars sat rusting in the rain as tall weeds pushed up through the tracks. The Long Path Express, I thought to myself, as I sat down on the concrete, took off my shoes, and wrung out the socks. Pulling out a pair of glasses, I examined my feet. There weren't any blisters, but the skin was heavily wrinkled, just as if I had been splashing around in a swimming pool all day. I rubbed my feet with balm and hung out for an hour, letting them dry out. It was around 2:00 a.m. and very quiet, except for an occasional car passing by.

Up and on my feet again, I followed the road past darkened houses, lawns, fields, forest. Always I kept one eye on the next telephone pole, seeking an aqua-colored confirmation that this was the right way. And now the road crossed over another highway, Interstate 84, which headed west into Pennsylvania. I paused on the overpass to marvel at the line of trucks barreling through the misty night. Moving forward once more on another country road, I looked up and the blazes were gone. After some brief confusion, the mapping function on my cellphone got me headed in the right direction again, with four long miles to go until the woods. As I put the phone away, I noticed the voicemail indicator was on. Whatever it was would have to wait. I wasn't in position to deal with issues from the outside world, and I wasn't about to let anything derail my quest.

A truck passed me several times. It was apparently delivering newspapers. The predawn light revealed an enormous mansion perched on the top of a ridge. One last paved mile brought me to the entrance of Ridgeview, a parcel of land purchased and set aside as a nature preserve by the Open Space Institute, and a return to the woods and softer trails.

It was time for a break. Once again, I unlaced shoes, wrung out wet socks, rubbed feet with balm, and gave them a few minutes to dry out, while I rehydrated a freeze-dried camping meal. The malodorous trash bag redeemed itself as a ground cloth. I leaned back to admire the early morning sky.

Since waking up the day before at Big Hill Lean-To, I had been on the move for twenty-three hours straight and during this time covered sixty miles, for an average pace of just over two-and-a-half miles per hour. Not very fast, what with half the distance on roads, but progress nonetheless.

I had ventured through the quiet valleys and past the billion-year-old rocky outcroppings of Harriman State Park, crossed a valley populated with small squeaking frogs, summitted Long and Schunemunk Mountains. In its peculiar manner, the Long Path had followed the cracked asphalt of an abandoned road, meandered along a gas-line right of way, ducked underneath an ancient train trestle, and crossed the Thruway, Routes 6 and 17 (the latter three times), and I-84. It was an eclectic combination, a reflection of how the Long Path's creators had navigated the sprawl of upstate New York while searching out areas of natural beauty. From here on out, however, the Long Path was headed into increasingly remote areas. There would be no more highways.

With 105 miles down, there were only 245 left to go—a distance still almost twice as long as anything I had ever done before. It's hard to get your mind around something like that, and I didn't try.

The first day on the Long Path had been easy. The second day had presented some challenges. No doubt, things would soon get even more interesting.

I closed my eyes for just a minute.

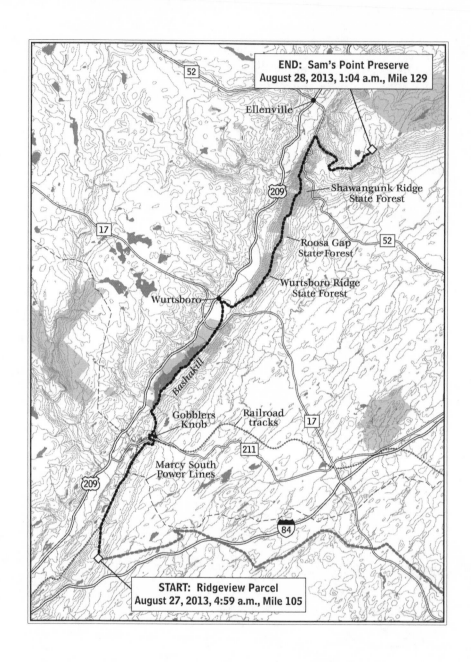

END: Sam's Point Preserve
August 28, 2013, 1:04 a.m., Mile 129

52

Ellenville

209

Shawangunk Ridge
State Forest

Roosa Gap
State Forest

52

17

Wurtsboro Ridge
State Forest

Wurtsboro

Bashakill

Gobblers
Knob

Railroad
tracks

17

211

Marcy South
Power Lines

84

209

START: Ridgeview Parcel
August 27, 2013, 4:59 a.m., Mile 105

Chapter 5

Half Moon and Cold Wind,
Two Thousand Feet Above the Valley Floor

Now I see the secret of the making of the best persons,
It is to grow in the open air and to eat and sleep with the earth.

—Walt Whitman, "Song of the Open Road"

Ridgeview Parcel, Mountain Road, Greenville, New York,
Tuesday, August 27, 2013, 4:59 a.m.

I woke with a start. A small mosquito had buzzed in my ear, bringing back unpleasant memories.

Earlier in the summer, I had ventured out this way for a training run. In a rush to pack, I had grabbed a bottle of all-natural bug spray, the kind that's made out of citronella or some other naturally occurring ingredient, rather than industrial-strength chemical toxins such as DEET. It was a poor choice. Maybe the all-natural stuff slowed down the mosquitoes. Maybe it even smelled bad to them. But it didn't stop them. They chased me up and over the ridgeline. I lost the Long Path and fled into the next valley. When I finally found a cellphone signal, I called my wife Sue requesting a tactical extraction, preferably by helicopter. She graciously agreed and arrived an hour later in the family car, Odie riding shotgun.

But on this morning, the mosquito flew off, and I lumbered to my feet, reassembled my kit, and was off as well.

The path followed a grassy woodlands road through a forest of mixed hardwoods. After a couple of minutes' confusion, where a gas-line right of way bisected the path, I regained my bearings and continued onward, passing a pond on the left. The path then meandered into a valley, paralleling what seemed to be an out-of-service railway line. A train materialized, startling me, and rattled down the tracks.

Now veering away from the active line, the path followed an abandoned railway bed strewn with large chunky cinders. The sharp rock edges pressed through the thin soles of my minimalist shoes. My feet began to ache, and my pace slowed.

After some time, the rail bed emerged onto an open ridge, where it was joined by the Marcy South Power Line, which brings hydroelectric power to southern New York from generation facilities in Canada. First proposed by the New York Power Authority in 1982, the project met with intense resistance as locals fretted about the impact of power lines on health, the environment, and property values. Farmers barred the power authority's surveyors from their properties, brandished firearms, and even vandalized equipment. But New York City needed electricity. The power authority responded to local resistance, not with the heavy-handed tactics of a Robert Moses, but rather by addressing health concerns, enlisting political support, and handing out millions of dollars of compensation for acquired land. The lines went operational in 1988.

The sun was now out, and I paused to apply sunblock and admire the power line's steel and concrete towers, which marched along the path like giant robots and then half a mile later turned downhill and strode across the valley and up the next ridge.

The path ducked back into the woods and then emerged at Route 211 near the town of Otisville. Out of nowhere a glass bottle came rolling slowly downhill on the pavement, its progress seemingly too deliberate for the slope. Eventually the bottle came to rest on the shoulder. I blinked in bewilderment.

After following the paved road for a quarter mile, the path turned off the pavement and headed up a steep trail to a hilltop called Gobblers Knob. But for its name, this seemed to be an uninteresting hilltop, indistinguishable from its many neighbors, and a gratuitous climb that made the Long Path a little bit longer than was strictly necessary. I dug in with the trekking poles, determined to get the ascent over and done with. From the top there was a view to the south of hills and forest, and a last glimpse of the towers of the Marcy South Power Line marching off into the distance.

The trail descended and after several switchbacks regained the paved road. I crossed to the far side and sat down in the grass next to the bank of the Bashakill, which was flowing clear and fast after emerging from an enormous wetland, the largest in southeastern New York.

It was time for breakfast. I filtered water from the river and rehydrated a freeze-dried camping meal. Off came squelchy shoes and socks. Out came wet feet. The skin was wrinkled and tender, but there were no blisters.

The camping meal was soon soggy enough to eat. According to the instructions, you were supposed to mix in hot water, but I wasn't about to carry the weight of a stove or wait for a pot to boil. Cold water would have to do. The package was labeled "corn and chili," and while it might have been almost anything as far as the taste and texture were concerned, it was good to get some calories. The sun peeked out from behind clouds, watery but warm. I wiggled my toes, cupped my hands behind my head, closed my eyes, and drifted off.

The Bashakill wetlands encompass three thousand acres in a wide valley through which the Bashakill winds back and forth. The area is reportedly home to two hundred varieties of birds, including geese, eagles, bitterns, herons, warblers, hawks, owls, and dozens of different duck species. On a prior visit, I had come through the wetlands at night, my progress marked by periodic splashes as creatures hopped and scurried out of the way, reminiscent of the small squeaking frogs in Harriman, although judging from the sounds, these were much larger. I had camped for a couple of hours on a dry section of the trail, listening to crickets, owls, and a mother deer barking for her young, before mosquitoes got me up and moving.

The sun was still shining. I stretched, then gathered my kit together. The trail continued along the same former rail bed, and the path was flat, smooth, reasonably straight, and well marked, on occasion crossing streams on stout wooden planks. To the left lay an immense field of reeds, shining emerald green in the sunlight. On the far side of the valley loomed a line of brilliant green hills. It felt like being in an immense green amphitheater. There was no sign of human habitation.

The sun was hot overhead, but the trail was shaded, and I trotted along comfortably for a few miles. Then the trail emerged into the open and became overgrown with tall grass. I slowed to a walk. There was a muddy section, and my shoes and socks were once again soaked.

After a little while, the path crossed underneath Route 17 (for the fourth and final time), the traffic overhead a muffled and distant reminder of the real world, and entered the outskirts of the little town of Wurtsboro. Back on paved roads, I made a determined effort to run the mile or so into town, tender feet complaining with every step.

Wurtsboro was named for William Wurts, a Philadelphia businessman who discovered anthracite coal in northeastern Pennsylvania during the early nineteenth century. Wurts bought land and dug mines, but found it was too costly to transport the ore back to Philadelphia. Instead, inspired by the success of the Eerie Canal, he and his two brothers came up with the idea of digging a 108-mile canal from the Pennsylvania coal fields to the Hudson River near the town of Kingston, New York, from which point barges could transport the coal to Albany and New York City. It took a long time to convince people that anthracite coal was a legitimate fuel source and to obtain enabling legislation in Pennsylvania and New York. It took only a single day, however, to raise $1.5 million in funding, which made the Delaware and Hudson Canal Company the first million-dollar private corporation in the United States. Construction was completed between 1825 and 1828.

At an 1827 jubilee in celebration of the soon-to-open canal, William's brother Maurice was lauded for his role in the routing and construction of the canal: "If we view him leaving the enjoyments of a refined city, alone and unknown, exploring the unfrequented valley, examining the various water courses, and climbing the rugged mountains which lie between the coal beds and the Hudson . . . and see him at length on Shawangunk's lofty summit, viewing with an eagle glance, a way to which reduce his long nursed vision to a happy reality, we must admit his conceptions were great, his design was grand."

In 1830, the canal carried a little under forty-four thousand tons of coal. In due course, this volume swelled to over one million tons of coal per year plus wood and other commodities. The canal also contributed to the growth of a series of small towns along its path, many of whose inhabitants worked on or for the canal. Remnants of the canal have been reclaimed as a linear park, which extends for a few miles from Wurtsboro northeast along the base of the Shawangunk Mountains, which the Long Path would soon ascend.

Downtown Wurtsboro is little more than an intersection, with two restaurants, two gas stations, and a handful of small stores and businesses. I stopped at the Stewart's for bottled water and a can of beer, then made my way down the street to San José's Café, a small Mexican restaurant with a single table on the sidewalk and a pair of flimsy plastic chairs. I sat down heavily. Determined to avoid junk food, I rejected hamburgers and tacos, compromising instead on a plate of French fries (in hindsight, the reasoning behind this choice isn't particularly clear). For the fifth time in the last twenty-four hours, I took off my shoes and socks and wrung out a quantity of dirty water. Then I placed them on the shoulder of the road to dry in the sun. There weren't any other customers. The waitress struck up a conversation. I chatted along, but kept a careful eye on shoes and socks, worried that a car might inadvertently park on top of them.

The French fries finished, I stood up to leave, wondering briefly if I had consumed enough calories. But the clock was ticking, and time was not going to wait for me to order another dish.

The Long Path took me out of Wurtsboro on a paved road, past the post office, auto repair shop, volunteer fire department, and a motorcycle dealership. Then it was up a steep hill, cars whizzing past uncomfortably close. The path turned onto a narrow trail in the woods and headed up onto the Shawangunk ridgeline.

The "Gunks" or the "Shongums," as the locals call them, are a mountain range stretching roughly seventy miles from High Point State Park in northern New Jersey all the way to the town of Rosendale in New York's Ulster County. The Gunks represent the westernmost edge of the Great Appalachian Valley, and the same geographical feature reaches further south, where it is known as Kittatinny Mountain in New Jersey, Blue Mountain in Pennsylvania, and North Mountain in Virginia.

Rising two thousand feet above the Hudson Valley plains, the Shawangunks dominate the countryside for miles around. People who live in the area are passionate about the distinctive landscape. Almost the entire ridgeline has been protected by a patchwork of parks and preserves, including High Point State Park, the Ridgeview Parcel, Huckleberry Ridge State Forest, Wurtsboro Ridge State Forest, Roosa Gap State Forest, Shawangunk Ridge State Forest, Sam's Point Preserve, Minnewaska State Park, Witch's Hole State Forest, and the Mohonk Preserve. This didn't happen by accident. The Open Space Institute, formed in 1974 to preserve significant landscapes in New York State, has played a decisive role in protecting the Shawangunks. OSI and its conservation partners, including the Trail Conference, the Nature Conservancy, and others, have spent upwards of $80 million to acquire over thirty-two-thousand acres of land in the Shawangunks. If it weren't for their efforts, this distinctive mountain range might be dotted with housing developments, gas stations, and shopping centers.

Part of what makes the mountains so distinctive is the shiny white rock called Shawangunk conglomerate of which they are composed. Five hundred million years ago, ancestral North America collided against an arc of islands, and the resulting volcanic activity created a range of mountains in eastern New York called the Taconics. Over the next hundred million years, the Taconics eroded, and the sediment was carried to the west, where it formed layers of Shawangunk conglomerate on top of strata of soft gray sandstone. About three hundred million years ago, during the period that geologists refer to as the Alleghenian orogeny (mountain-building event), ancestral Africa crushed against North America, buckling the earth's crust into a system of mountain ranges, today known broadly as the Appalachians, which ripple across the landscape from Alabama to Maine. During this period, long plates of Shawangunk conglomerate were deformed and tilted upward. On the eastern edge of the Shawangunk range, these plates are broken and eroded, forming an escarpment of cliffs, ledges, and outcroppings. On the western side, the plateau slopes gently toward the valley floor. Viewed from the north or south, the mountain range looks like an enormous green wave, cresting to the east, where it breaks into a foam of white cliffs and boulders.

The cliffs are white because Shawangunk conglomerate consists of quartz pebbles cemented together by silica. In some spots, the rocks have been weathered to a light gray or covered in lichens brown, black, and green, but in others, especially where the rocks were scoured by glaciers, they gleam white. Under a full moon, they seem to glow in the dark.

I had run in the Shawangunk Mountains for almost twenty years. I had run in the scrub oak forests and dwarf pine barrens, through the stunted, twisted trees that grow on the thin soil of the summits. I had wandered through endless blueberry and huckleberry heath and seen the bushes flowering in the spring, the berries ripening under the summer sun, and the leaves turning claret and rust in the fall. I knew the meadows, lakes, and ponds, the mountain laurel with its sprays of delicate white and pink blossoms, the groves of hemlock where the paths are covered in soft needles.

Odie often accompanied me. He would chase after deer with boundless enthusiasm, but never quite catch them (it's not fair, his expression seemed to say—they jump *over* the fallen trees, while I must run *around* them). We saw porcupines, rattlesnakes, grouse, red-tailed hawks, vultures, and black bear. (Odie was game to go after the bears—it was only with great reluctance that he agreed not to.)

We had run along these paths in the heat of the summer, in the pouring rain, through thick mist, in the fall when the maples turned brilliant orange, the beeches and hickories yellow, the sumacs red, the oaks warm brown. In the winter we had battled through snowdrifts and skidded across ice-covered rocks to stand high on the plateau and gaze out across a tapestry of gray woods, tan fields, and blue hills.

For all my experience with the Shawangunks, the truth was I had spent most of my time in the northern sections. As I headed up the slope into Wurtsboro Ridge State Forest, I followed the blazes carefully. The sun was high in the sky, and I drank continuously from the camelback. The trail crossed rocks ledges of shiny white conglomerate, and then plunged into a forested ravine. From the top, there were views back toward the Bashakill wetlands. Down at the base of the ridge, looking odd and out of place in the rural countryside, sat a large distribution warehouse with rows of loading docks, and next to it a small airstrip. Between these structures and the ridge lay the former Delaware and Hudson Canal.

The white conglomerate rocks sparkle in the sunlight, but they become treacherous when wet. As a general rule, when running across rocks, you must pay close attention to the angle of your foot and the camber of the surface on which your foot lands. It's generally a good idea to point your toes in the direction of the slope, so that if you lose traction, you fall forward or back, but not off to the side. With practice, you learn to anticipate what might happen if a rock tilts under your step or if your foot slips out from underneath you.

On an earlier run, I had crossed this section in the morning, and noting the dew shining on the rock faces, I was proceeding carefully, especially on the sections where the rock face slanted away to the side. Despite my caution, I slipped and fell, but caught myself with an arm and knee against the ground. Pulling myself back up, I move forward with extra caution. And then fell again. Now it was time to get serious, and I was proceeding over the slippery rocks with great alertness (although it was hard not to admire the views)—when my feet slipped out from under me and flew off to the side. I fell heavily on my rear end and let loose a bellow of rage, sure that something was broken. This was not the case, but I did end up with a large bruise on my butt.

This time around, the rocks were dry, but even so I proceeded with extreme vigilance until off the ridge and back onto a dirt pathway in the woods.

Toward dusk, the trail passed into the Shawangunk Ridge State Forest, a section of the ridgeline I had never before visited. After a steep climb, the trail leveled out and was wide and neatly trimmed. On a little knob there was an old sign posted on a tree. A typewritten sheet was framed in light blue painted wood and protected by a blurry piece of acrylic. I peered at the text. Apparently, this was a memorial for a person named Jack Hennessy, a volunteer "maintainer," that is, someone responsible for trimming the vegetation, removing deadfall, and otherwise keeping clear this section of the trail. From what I could decipher of the faded text, Jack had started working on this trail upon retirement in 1992 and continued to do so until within two weeks of his death from cancer. Later on, I would learn from a friend that his ashes had been scattered along the trail. He was remembered as a "dedicated volunteer, a perfect example of the selfless worker—someone you could call on to do anything at short notice, but who never made you feel guilty." It was also noted that in 1994, he had walked the entire Long Path, then 236 miles.

Evidently Jack's passion for the land and the hard work he put into its care had made an impression. This section of the trail had been trimmed recently. His successors must have been similarly dedicated. Or perhaps his spirit watched over this part of the trail, which was one of his favorite spots on the ridge. But the next section of the trail had not been maintained recently. Shoulder-high scrub oak crowded in on me and scratched my legs as I pushed through.

Then the trail dipped into a saddle and passed a series of old stone walls. Whatever habitations had once existed here, they were long since gone. The fields couldn't have been prosperous, in this dark glen and rocky soil. Now they were ghost farms.

Nearing another summit along the ridge, I glimpsed snatches of light through the scrub oak. The trail then reached a series of conglomerate boulders and meandered back and forth along the edge of a short cliff, rocks covered with brown and black lichen, the trail overgrown in places with wavy grass, the forest below lying in deepening shadow. There were some views to the south, and then glimpses of Sam's Point to the north. A vulture was turning overhead. As I looked up at the views, then down at my feet, then around for the next blaze, I found the experience dizzying, and it was difficult to keep track of direction. The trail seemed to loop back and forth madly. The sun descended through a swirl of clouds and set in a burst of color. An ancient, gnarled dwarf pine tree stood near the top, a blaze painted on its trunk, one branch extended, like a weird hag beckoning me forward. The path dropped down a steep slope. The light dimmed. A snatch of music drifted in the air, but there weren't any houses or lights to be seen.

The trail now turned onto an old highway, a ghost of a road abandoned ages ago, the surface deeply eroded and strewn with large rocks that hurt my feet. It was pitch black, and I moved forward cautiously, the course notes clutched in one hand, flashlight in the other, panning around for the next aqua blaze, trying not to stumble on the stones. Two-and-a-half miles on this road seemed an eternity. There was no way to gauge progress, except by counting steps. A stream cut a deep channel across the road before pouring down the mountain. I became disoriented. After turning in circles a few times, I picked up the blazes again. Now I had lost count of my steps. There was no way to pinpoint my location on this ancient road or estimate when it would end. I pushed on through the darkness. My journey seemed endless.

A car could be heard passing by overhead and to the right. A few steps later, the old road reached Route 52, a two-lane highway outside Ellenville, a small town on the far side of the ridge. I stepped onto the asphalt and breathed a sigh of relief.

In the late nineteenth century, during the heyday of the Delaware and Hudson Canal, Ellenville was a thriving town with a population of three thousand, up from the three families reported living there prior to the canal's construction. Its inhabitants included boatmen and crews, lock tenders, boat builders, and others employed directly and indirectly in the work of the canal. The canal had also provided a means to export goods to market, and Ellenville boasted productive farms and manufacturing, including a glassworks and cutlery and axe factories. The eventual demise of the canal left Ellenville stranded. Its population today is just over four thousand, and like many small towns in upstate New York, it struggles to attract industry. It does, however, offer a well-regarded theater, some excellent restaurants, and several hang-gliding schools, whose participants launch themselves into thermal eddies from the heights of the Shawangunk Ridge, alongside vultures, hawks, and eagles.

I hadn't studied the map for this section of the Long Path, assuming the path would follow a paved road to Sam's Point Preserve. After all, I knew there was such a road. Why wouldn't the Long Path take the easiest and most direct route?

But besides Route 52, there were no other roads in sight. The notes instructed me to walk along Route 52 for 0.05 mile. I struggled to process that information. How far was 0.05 miles? I couldn't decide whether it was a hop, skip, and jump or an endless trek in the dark. Crossing Route 52, I followed a steel guiderail, looking around for a road. Not finding one, I doubled back and tried again, then sat down on the ground and tried to make sense of the situation. Eventually I spotted a Long Path disk nailed to a tree a few yards in from the highway. Aqua blazes marked a narrow footpath heading uphill and into the woods.

According to the map, the elevation gain from Route 52 to Sam's Point totals twelve hundred feet. Indeed, the trail was soon climbing upward at a steep pitch, hugging the right-hand side of a deep ravine. Far, far below in the darkness came the sound of rushing water. I toiled upward. Once again the camelback was empty, and I was suddenly quite thirsty, but the ravine plunged too steeply, and the water was far too distant to reach. I dug in with the trekking poles, while the trail continued to rise.

At one point I paused to catch my breath, and looking down saw a small black salamander covered with silver spots, stationary on the path, as if it were basking in the starlight. Thoreau had once encountered this species, which he described as a "sluggish portentous and outlandish spotted salamander, a trace of Egypt and the Nile." I stared at this magical creature for a few moments before heading on.

Now the sound of water was closer to the path. With great care, I stepped off the trail, maneuvered through the long branches of some large conifers, glancing repeatedly over my shoulder, trying to fix an impression of the trail's location in the thick darkness. If you lost the trail in these circumstances, you'd have a problem: even if you stumbled across the trail again, you might not recognize it, unless you spotted a blaze, because the pathway is so rough and indistinct. No doubt you'd find yourself again sometime the next morning—having had the chance to appreciate the "vastness and strangeness of nature," as Thoreau had observed. But the experience would not be conducive to setting a fastest-known time.

After struggling down into the base of the ravine, I found the stream, refilled the camelback, and then groped my way back up to the path. As it turned out, in a few hundred yards, the path crossed a secondary stream, where I could have refilled without the risk of venturing off course.

The trail eventually reached a paved road. I looked around for blazes, but saw nothing. I've since been back to this spot in the daylight and found the blazes clearly pointing into the woods on the far side of the road, after a hundred-yard jog to the left. But in the darkness, I missed the blazes and failed to find any signs of the path, even after marching up and down the road a quarter-mile in each direction shining my flashlight in all directions. The mapping function on my cellphone indicated that this road would lead in a mile and half to the Sam's Point visitor center, where I knew the Long Path would continue. After giving up on the blazes, I headed out along the paved road, feeling apprehensive. At night, when one is tired, errors are easy. Everything must be double-checked and second-guessed. I waved down a passing car, demanding to know if this was the road to Sam's Point. They said it was.

Thirty minutes later, Sam's Point was in sight, the parking lot deserted, a solitary light burning in the visitor center. A prominent sign stated that the park closed at dusk. It was now midnight. I made my way discretely along the edge of the parking lot, trying to look nonchalant, as if I belonged here at this late hour. I started to worry that security cameras might be tracking my progress. Undoubtedly the people in the car I had waved down had already reported a suspicious character abroad in the night. Unnerved, I slunk quietly through the shadows, rehearsing an explanation for this trespass and hoping the police wouldn't drag me off in handcuffs. (In hindsight, this episode is an example of how sleep deprivation can intensify ordinary caution into paranoid anxiety.)

Aqua blazes reappeared at the far end of the parking lot and followed a carriage trail up and onto the side of the ridge. After a little while, the Long Path veered off from the carriage trail onto a narrow footpath, strewn with rocks, the white Shawangunk conglomerate glowing dimly in the darkness.

A large orange dot hung in the night sky, just above the horizon. Mesmerized, I stared at this phenomenon for several minutes. Clouds blew by, revealing the rest of the half-moon. The clouds kept moving across the sky, and the moon was soon covered again.

Down below, the darkened valley floor was speckled with lights arrayed in complex, hieroglyphic patterns. I couldn't figure out which small towns they belonged to, even though I surely knew them all.

It was now past one in the morning, and I was tired. I had been on the move for forty hours straight, trying desperately to stay on schedule—despite rain, tender feet, mud, steep hills, and rocks both slippery and sharp. My pace had slowed significantly, and despite all the effort I had fallen a full twelve hours behind plan.

I'd made it 129 miles so far; the remaining distance was too much to think about. I wanted to keep going, to try to make up lost time. But my concentration was wavering. I stumbled upon the gleaming white rocks, wobbling with fatigue.

I dragged myself forward until the trail offered just enough space to stretch out between the conglomerate debris. Spreading the poncho liner on the damp ground, I wrapped myself in it as snugly as possible. The valley floor lay two thousand feet below, and up here the winds were cold. I woke up from time to time, shifted position, and cinched the poncho liner tightly about me.

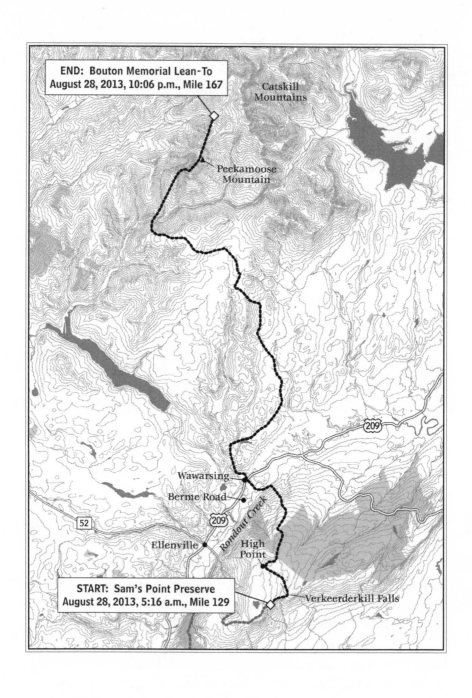

END: Bouton Memorial Lean-To
August 28, 2013, 10:06 p.m., Mile 167

Catskill
Mountains

Peekamoose
Mountain

209

Wawarsing

Berme Road

52

209

Rondout Creek

Ellenville

High
Point

START: Sam's Point Preserve
August 28, 2013, 5:16 a.m., Mile 129

Verkeerderkill Falls

Chapter 6

Silence and Darkness

Forever alive, forever forward,
Stately, solemn, sad, withdrawn, baffled, mad, turbulent, feeble,
   dissatisfied,
Desperate, proud, fond, sick, accepted by men, rejected by men,
They go! they go! I know that they go, but I know not where
   they go,
But I know that they go toward the best—toward something great.

     —Walt Whitman, "Song of the Open Road"

Sam's Point Nature Preserve, Wednesday, August 28, 2013, 5:16 a.m.

It was the gray light before dawn, and the air was thick with mist. Shivering, I packed up and moved out. There was a long ways to go, and treacherous terrain ahead.

For now I was on familiar ground, having run this section of the trail earlier in the summer. Back then, I had paused near here, high above the Hudson Valley, and surveyed the length and breadth of the Shawangunk Mountains. I had followed the spine of the ridge with my eyes, tracing with outstretched hand its descent past Wurtsboro and the Bashakill wetlands, all the way into New Jersey, some forty miles away to the southwest. Wheeling about to the northeast, I had tracked the ridgeline as it spiraled lazily past waterfalls, sky lakes, and cliff faces, all the way to a stone tower called Skytop that stands on one of the northernmost summits, nearly thirty miles distant. The enormity of my journey seemed almost within grasp. David O'Neill, the man who first ran the Long Path, expressed a similar reaction to this place. He reported that he had been awed by the beauty of the Shawangunks more than any other place, because he could see where he had come from and where he was headed.

But this morning the air was misty, and there was no view. The trail consisted of a jumble of hard, angular conglomerate rocks. Between the rocks, the dirt was laced with roots. The path led through dwarf pine barrens and past blueberry bushes growing shoulder high, before dipping into a grove of birch and rhododendron. I hopped across a stream that had cut a narrow channel in the sandstone shelf, not pausing to peer over the edge where the water plunges onto rocks 180 feet below. This is Verkeerderkill Falls. Nailed to a tree, a wooden sign announces, "You are entering one of Earth's last great places."

A little while later, the Long Path reached an intersection with a red-blazed trail, turned left, and angled up toward the top of the ridge. Earlier in the summer I had encountered a Trail Conference volunteer here who was trimming the blueberry bushes and making the trail wider and easier to navigate. I had thanked him for his work.

As it headed upward, the trail followed a series of rock ledges above the floor of a broad gully populated with dwarf pine and paper birch. Somewhere in the depths the Verkeerderkill Creek was flowing toward the falls.

In some places, the Shawangunk conglomerate had been polished by ancient glaciers, and the rock face showed the characteristic striations (parallel lines) and chatter marks (crescent-shaped grooves) where ice had dragged boulders across. Elsewhere, the rock was covered with soft gray-green or flaky brown-black lichen. The footing alternated between bare rock, pine needles, and gray sand. As the trail ascended farther up the mountain, the trees became shorter until the dwarf pine stood only waist high, with tentacle-like branches curling among the rocks.

I reached a large white rocky outcropping just as the sun was rising and the mist was clearing. At 2,289 feet, High Point is indeed the highest point in the Shawangunks. Below me, the ridge spread into a broad plateau, and the dwarf-pine barrens stretched for miles; it was as if I were sitting in a white boat bobbing on a deep green sea. The views here are endless. On a clear day, I'm told you can look to the west and see Mount Ararat in the Moosic Mountains of Pennsylvania, sixty miles away. These mountains mark the origin of the Delaware and Hudson Canal and the coal fields which it served. Fifty miles to the east stands Mount Everett in Massachusetts's Berkshire Mountains. On a very clear day, you might see Mount Greylock, the tallest mountain in Massachusetts, 89 miles distant, and possibly glimpse Mount Equinox, near Manchester, Vermont, 119 miles to the northeast.

But as soon as you lift your eyes from the plateau, the Catskill Mountains command your attention, looming above the valley in elemental splendor. Remote, rugged, massive, the peaks both beckon and threaten. The Shawangunks now seem insignificant. To the northeast, Skytop tower looks no bigger than a pebble.

Three hundred fifty million years ago, the Catskill Delta, as it is now called by geologists, consisted of swamps, shallow ponds, and twisting streams, stretching from New York as far west as Ohio, and simmering under a tropical sun. To the east stood the Acadians, another prehistoric mountain range, created during the so-called Acadian orogeny roughly four hundred million years ago, when ancestral Europe collided with North America. When first thrust up from the Earth's crust, the Acadians may have towered thirty thousand feet into the sky. Over time, the Acadians eroded, and the sediment drained to the west, accumulating in the Catskill Delta as layers of dark red shale and gray sandstone.

Roughly three hundred million years ago, the forces unleashed during the Alleghenian orogeny (when ancestral North America and Africa collided to produce the Appalachians) not only folded and tilted the Shawangunks, but uplifted the Catskill Delta into a massive plateau. Over time the action of water and ice carved the plateau into the series of rocky peaks, which today are called the Catskill Mountains.

By the time the Catskills were uplifted, the Acadian Mountains were long gone. Today, virtually no trace of them remains but for the gentle Berkshires of western Massachusetts. Ironically, what was once a low-lying delta now rises above the mountains from which it was formed.

I stared long and hard at the Catskills. To my left, on the western side of the plateau, Slide Mountain reared up from behind a circle of lower peaks. I was supposed to reach this general area some time tonight. Thirty miles away, it seemed impossibly distant. After Slide Mountain, I would turn northeast, drop into a narrow valley, and make my way to the small town of Phoenicia. From there, the path would take me up into the mountains again, heading farther east along a steep mountain rampart with deep clefts between peaks. Along this craggy ridge, the Long Path coincides with the Devil's Path, so named by early settlers, who believed the Devil had specially built these rocky cliffs so that he alone could climb them when he sought refuge from the world of men.

From the Shawangunks, this jagged mountain wall shimmers electric blue against the horizon. Locals call it the "million-dollar view." It is indeed a beautiful sight, but traversing it would be different from admiring it. I had been on the Devil's Path once, many years ago. I didn't remember much besides incessant climbing and deep fatigue.

It was time to take on the Catskills, but before leaving High Point, I turned around one last time, trying to absorb the views. They stretched out in all directions for seemingly infinite distances. To the east, farms lay scattered across the Hudson Valley, and beyond them a shadow marked where Schunemunk Mountain and the Hudson Highlands rose above the river. To the south, past the broad plains of the Wallkill River, the ancient ridges of Harriman State Park appeared as a dark wave. Big Hill Lean-To, the Torrey memorial, and the valley of the frogs seemed such a long time ago. To the west, the sky gleamed along the horizon. I took a deep breath and departed.

Descending from High Point, the trail followed the long, gradually sloping backside of the plateau, winding between blueberry, rhododendron, dwarf pine, birch, hemlock, and sassafras. Until the 1950s, this area was frequented by itinerant berry pickers. According to the notes, there were still a couple of shacks left where they lived during the summer, but I didn't look for them. Instead, I kept my head down as I moved across the shiny white conglomerate rock faces, fearful that the morning dew might have left them slippery. Happily, I did not fall.

Eventually the path dropped down a steep hillside and reached Berme Road, a strip of asphalt deep in the forest. My third drop bag was waiting just where I had stashed it, about one hundred yards in from the trailhead. Four days ago, when I had driven here to cache the bag, I had had a devil of a time finding the trail. I had passed back and forth several times, staring through the windshield at aqua blazes painted on trees, but missing the trailhead. Eventually I found it, marked discretely with Long Path disks nailed to the trees about five yards in from the road. If you didn't know where to look, you'd never know a path was there. Portals to parallel universes are rarely conspicuous.

The Long Path now followed Berme Road along the valley floor under the shade of maple, oak, and hickory trees. To the side of the road lay a narrow ditch filled with muddy water. Here and there, stone facing was visible between the ditch and the banks of the Rondout Creek, which wound through the forest in broad loops. At the height of its operations, the Delaware and Hudson Canal measured fifty feet across at the top, thirty-two feet at the bottom, and six feet deep. More than one thousand wooden boats holding up to 140 tons of coal each moved slowly over the water, towed by teams of two or three horses. With an annual capacity that exceeded one million tons, the canal was for a time one of the most important transport arteries on the east coast. By the 1880s, however, railroad lines had reached New York City, offering lower costs than the canal, and operating not just in the summer but also during the winter, when the canal was frozen and impassable. The Delaware and Hudson Canal Company gradually shifted its coal from boats to railcars. To economize, the company cut boatman wages until these workers were subsisting on the brink of poverty. In 1899, the board of directors resolved to cease operations of the canal. The accountants wrote the book value down from $6 million (which represented the cumulative investment in creating and enlarging the canal over the preceding seventy-five years) to $100,000. A few months later, the company sold the canal for $10,000. The buyer used it to transport stone for the construction of Ulster Correctional Facility, a massive gothic structure and a brooding presence that sits along Berme Road on the outskirts of Ellenville. In 1901, the canal was abandoned for good. Where I was now standing, a narrow ditch filled with stagnant water was all that remained. In most other places, there is no visible sign left at all.

Meanwhile, my waterlogged feet began to complain again, and I grimaced at being back on the unforgiving asphalt. For a moment, though, I forgot about the discomfort as the road passed through a small valley with extensive corn fields glowing golden in the late morning light. A half-mile later, the road reached Route 208 on the outskirts of the hamlet of Wawarsing, and now I scanned the handful of buildings clustered around the intersection, searching for restaurants or a deli, even a gas station—anything that might offer a snack. But there was nothing. Disappointed, I crossed Route 208 and kept going.

After another mile, it was time to pull up on the side of the road to let the feet dry out once again. My shoes seemed quick to absorb moisture, slow to dry. Foot powder and extra socks—standard operating procedures for Army Rangers—would have been a good idea. I munched on some food, swatted at a mosquito, and watched a delivery truck zoom by.

Over the next few miles, the road went from pavement to dirt to pavement again. In one area, the woods echoed with the roar of machinery for a long time before I finally came upon large rollers flattening the dirt. I gave them wide berth. Next the road passed a curious compound. From between slats in a twelve-foot-tall wooden wall, a large house and lawn were intermittently visible, and the sounds of country music wafted along the breeze. On the other side of the road, an old cemetery lay moldering in the woods.

I walked for a bit, then tried to resume a slow jog. When I'm tired, I make a point to focus on form, and sometimes that helps me keep moving more efficiently. Lift your chest, tilt your hips just a little forward while keeping the natural curve in your back, sink ever so slightly downward, and raise the knees. Do this and a brisk walk turns into a slow jog. You might accelerate by one mile per hour. Doesn't seem like much, but over ten miles it could save you thirty minutes. Over a hundred miles, it might save you six hours. A new record might turn on such thin margins.

It began to rain. I forgot about form and instead eyed the porches, barns, and garages along the side of the road. A bench situated in a perennial garden looked especially inviting. But the clock was not going to stop ticking while I sat down for a break.

After a few more miles, the pavement ended at the entrance to a state forest preserve. The path now plunged into deep woods and leapt forward along a snowmobile trail, which was wide and well-marked. A few minutes later the trail reached a low waterfall where the Vernooy Kill cascades over a series of dark rock ledges. According to the notes, the path was supposed to continue along another snowmobile trail for approximately one mile before turning off onto a footpath. I had been here once before, but couldn't remember where the turnoff was or whether it was clearly marked. If I missed it, the error would not necessarily be apparent until I reached the end of the snowmobile trail, however distant that might be.

After walking for a couple of minutes, I began to fret. Had I already missed the turnoff? Just to be safe, I turned around and backtracked half a mile toward the waterfall, then faced about and moved forward again. This time I scanned the brush closely for signs of a footpath, just in case the turnoff wasn't obvious. There were no such signs, however. Perhaps I hadn't gone back far enough. It felt like a mile already. I was just about to turn back once more and retreat all the way back to the waterfall to start again, this time counting every footstep along the way—when a large sign marked "Trail" came into view, with an arrow pointing to the left. The sign was so prominent and seemed so earnest in its effort to forestall confusion that I felt stupid for having forgotten it.

Although I hadn't remembered the sign, I recalled all too clearly the treacherous terrain waiting for me on the next section of the Long Path. Sure enough, after a few steps, I came across a large oak tree, easily two feet in diameter, lying across the trail. In falling, it had dragged down a pair of maple trees, and the three trunks created a kind of balustrade across the path. I stepped onto the oak, levered myself across the two maples, and lowered myself back onto the trail, trekking poles hanging from wrist-straps and clattering uselessly over the branches.

Hurricane Irene had struck New York almost exactly two years ago, and the violent weather must have spawned a tornado in this area. Presumably the New York State Department of Environmental Conservation knew of this debris and either didn't have the resources to clear it away or had prioritized other projects ahead of it. Or maybe, the earnest sign notwithstanding, no one ever came out this way, and the DEC didn't even know.

There was another bundle of downed trees, and again I climbed carefully over them. The next obstacle was so large and tangled that climbing over didn't seem feasible; instead I veered off the trail, pushing brush and saplings out of the way, until I had passed the base of an enormous tree which had been ripped from the ground, its broken roots exposed above a gaping crater of mud and rocks.

This section of the Long Path was marked with blue plastic disks. I headed into the deepening gloom, searching for signs of blue. It was raining steadily now.

More fallen trees. This time there must have been six or seven twisted together. I bushwhacked around the obstacle only to encounter more downed trees, requiring yet another detour deeper into the forest. I inched my way through the brush toward where the trail surely must lie. But there were no blue disks in sight. They might have been on the fallen trees, the blue plastic now crushed into the dirt. I pushed forward in what seemed the most likely direction. After a moment I found the next disk.

I counted thirty downed trees before losing track. Now there were easily a dozen great trees that had toppled with branches interlaced, like wrestlers locked in a clinch who continue to grapple even as they fall to the mat. I worked my way around in a counterclockwise direction, but couldn't locate the trail. Disoriented, I retreated to the last blue disk and pulled out my compass. Then I turned around and as I did so glanced out across the forest floor. To my surprise, it was clear of debris. Trees had been knocked down across the Long Path only, as if specifically to block the way.

By the time I reached the next turn on the trail, stepping across a final prostrate trunk, it seemed that I had crossed a hundred fallen trees. I took a deep breath, slowly let it out, and put the compass away.

The next leg of the Long Path followed a dirt road. There were no obstacles but rocks and mud. Frogs hopped out of the way, taking cover in nearby puddles. The larger ones stood their ground and watched me pass, faces expressionless, skin electric green and shimmering.

With the deadfall behind, my adrenaline dropped back to normal levels. So did my energy and focus. The clock be damned, it was time for a break. I pulled out the evil-smelling garbage bag, draped it over my body, leaned back against a tree, and closed my eyes.

A sudden movement awakened me. I thought it was a deer. No, a solitary mountain biker. I bolted upright; he grunted in surprise and kept peddling.

I trudged on. After a mile, the trail came upon a house tucked into the woodline. It was old and rickety, as if built of driftwood. The yard was strewn with boxes and rusting metal. The eaves were festooned with lights, although they were not illuminated. Why a house was standing here, in the middle of a state forest, was a mystery. Perhaps it predated the creation of the preserve. In the steady rain, the porch looked inviting. No one appeared to be home. But suppose the owner returned and discovered me asleep? Judging from the character of the house, he would be old and odd and not necessarily friendly. I kept going.

The trail headed uphill, crisscrossing through an ancient forest. There were beds of emerald ferns glistening with beads of water. The grass was knee-high and iridescent. I crossed a stream by stepping on mossy rocks. The air was thick with moisture and suffused with a dim light. The birds were quiet; the air was still. As in a great cathedral, there was a hushed reverence, a feeling that time could move no faster than the pace at which water droplets rolled off the leaves.

Eventually, the path crested the top of a ridge and then dropped steeply down the far side. The descent burned off one thousand feet of elevation in just over half a mile, straight downhill without any switch-backs, making the average grade close to 40 percent. I trotted downhill, dodging rocks and roots, quads absorbing the shock of each footfall. The descent was exhilarating. I reached bottom a few minutes later and arrived at a paved road, feeling spent. I shook my head and hurried along the road, following faded aqua blazes painted intermittently on trees.

And now it was time to face the next section of treacherous terrain and, I hoped, the last obstacle for today. The map showed the trail ascending along a knife-edged ridge to the summit of Peekamoose Mountain. Along this ridge, the path would climb twenty-five hundred feet over three miles, for an average grade of 16 percent.

To fortify myself for this challenge, I sat down on a large rock and ate some food. Mercifully the rain had stopped, although the sky remained overcast. Somewhere beyond the clouds, the sun was dropping behind mountain walls. The light was slowly fading.

At first the trail headed uphill at a moderate grade. The surface was brown clay strewn with round stones from some ancient streambed that no doubt dated back to the last ice age. It was dark now, and I clicked on my headlamp, swung my legs, and dug in with the trekking poles.

The path began to scramble up and around large boulders and through clefts in rock ledges. I reached an embankment, where the path split to the left and right. I chose the right fork. The path petered out. Up the slope and through some trees, a blue disk glinted in the headlamp's light. I grasped at roots and branches and pulled myself up and over a rock wall, then clambered over a fallen tree.

According to the map, the ridgeline fell away steeply to the left and right. Outside the headlamp's cone of light, everything was black. The trail flattened out for a moment. Then it surged upward along a crude staircase of dirt and rocks.

At some point, the trail leveled off and became sandy. Then there was a patch of mud. A triangular sandstone conglomerate boulder marked the top of Peekamoose. But there was no view. The trail was hemmed in on both sides by fir trees; it was like moving through a tunnel. After another period of time, and a short, steep downhill, I found myself standing in front of the Bouton Memorial Lean-To. It was a little after 10 p.m.

It had been a long day. In seventeen hours, I had covered thirty-eight miles—slightly more than two miles per hour. A miserable pace. But I had traversed some difficult terrain. I had gone up and over the Shawangunk Ridgeline, followed roads for twelve long miles, scrambled over, through, and around a monstrous barrier of downed trees, penetrated into the forest's silent heart, careened down a thousand-foot slope, then scaled Peekamoose in the dark.

From the three-blazed tree in Fort Lee Historic Park to the Bouton Memorial Lean-To, I had covered 167 miles. It didn't occur to me that night, but this spot was only eight miles short of the halfway point. It was just as well not to think of such things. In my ultraracing experience, getting to the halfway point is the easy part. Halfway in terms of distance does not mean halfway in terms of time or effort. Or pain. The second half is always harder than the first. The second half is where things go wrong.

I unbuckled my gear and lay down, trying to accommodate hips and shoulders to the hard wooden floor. What might lie ahead didn't matter right now. Sheltered from the elements by three walls and a roof, I was quickly asleep.

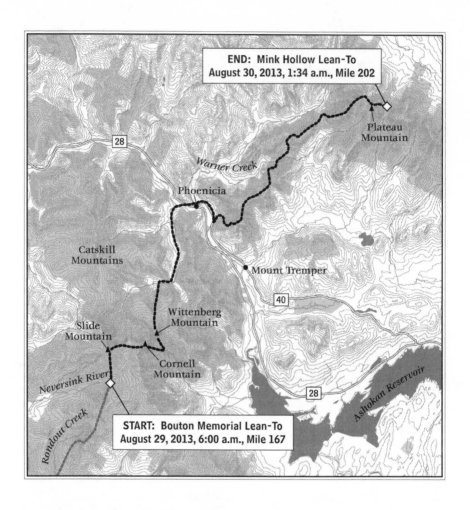

Chapter 7

Views from the Mountains, Voices from the Past

Now I re-examine philosophies and religions,
They may prove well in lecture-rooms, yet not prove at all under
    the spacious clouds and along the landscape and flowing currents.

—Walt Whitman, "Song of the Open Road"

Bouton Memorial Lean-To, Thursday, August 29, 2013, 6:00 a.m.

I awoke to find myself deep in the Catskills, 700,000 acres of rugged forest and mountain, roughly half state-owned forest preserve and wilderness area and half privately owned. After extensive logging, the state-owned land was set aside in 1895 together with the Adirondack Mountains as "forever wild" under Article 14 of the New York State Constitution. Before the loggers arrived, however, the Catskills had an unfavorable reputation. Native Americans avoided the area, preferring to dwell in the river valleys, where game was abundant and crops could be sown. White settlers also shunned the Catskills, fearful of witches, evil spirits, and terrible beasts. The rocky soil, steep terrain, and cool temperatures discouraged all but the poorest tenant farmers.

Having lived in New York for twenty years, I was somewhat familiar with the Catskills. Sue and I had ventured to the mountains soon after we were married for a weekend of hiking and a stay at a quaint bed and

85

breakfast. A few years later, young children in hand, we returned for a series of family camping trips. As time went by, camping fell out of favor, and instead we'd head to the Catskills for skiing and snowboarding. My introduction to trail racing took place in the northern Catskills, on the difficult Escarpment Trail.

Like many people, my initial impression of the Catskills was that the area's best times were behind it. A popular tourist destination in the nineteenth century, the Catskills subsequently fell in status. The region enjoyed a temporary renaissance with Jewish families in the 1950s. But since then, the tide of popularity had receded again, leaving behind a collection of very small towns, some bungalow colonies, and a variety of oddities, rather like fish stranded on the sand bed of a dying lake. Driving west from the Thruway on Route 28, I would marvel at the Dollhouse Museum and the World's Largest Indoor Kaleidoscope. Increasingly der-elict over the years, both had eventually closed. Still open is Fabulous Furniture, which sells fantastic sculptures welded together from junkyard car parts, including rocket ships and life-sized dinosaurs. Then there is the Emerson, an upscale resort notable for the larger-than-life panthers carved on its highway signage. At night, their eyes glow. Skirting the northern shoulders of the Catskills, Route 23 leads in quick succession past an abandoned gas station, a vacant motel, and then a large restau-rant with expansive views across Catskill Creek, recently foreclosed-upon despite a fresh coat of paint. Down the road stands a building whose balcony and roof are festooned with two-foot tall wooden bears wearing goggles and toting plastic M-16s.

But when you leave behind the sparse human settlements and ven-ture into the mountains, you discover a wilderness that is ancient, rugged, and hauntingly quiet.

ᴄᴡ

From the lean-to, I followed the trail as it made a long descent through a forest of yellow birch, ferns, and moss-covered logs, with tiny red mushrooms poking out along the side of the path. The trail dropped through a field of boulders, then passed over the headwaters of the Neversink River on a pair of stoutly built wooden bridges, one with railings, the other with a steel cable to hold for balance. Strictly speaking, this location lies outside the Hudson Valley, as the Neversink drains southwest into the Delaware River, but that doesn't mean it's beyond the grasp of New York City's water supply system. Before it reaches the Delaware, the Neversink is impounded in a reservoir, from which a significant volume of water flows through an eighty-five-mile-long aqueduct that tunnels underneath the Shawangunk Mountains on its way to the thirsty metropolis.

Now it was back uphill, along an interminable trail of red-brown clay, the path strewn with rocks and hard on the feet. I passed boulders composed of many thin layers of stone, looking like pages of a giant book, no doubt sediment deposited in the sultry swamps of the Catskill Delta some four hundred million years ago.

The forest was quiet, the silence broken from time to time by a bird, but the calls sounded distant and tentative. Otherwise it was still. Down below in the valleys, crickets, katydids, and cicadas produce endless cacophony. But up here, besides the occasional fly, the insect life seems subdued. Down below, squirrels and chipmunks cavort through dry leaves, rustling them so loudly you'd think they were bears. Up here, one senses a furtive footstep, catches a dash of movement out of the corner of the eye, and then it's silent again.

As it neared the top of the ridge, the path straightened out and then was smooth, flat, and covered in white sand, much like a garden walkway. After a short distance, I arrived at the summit of Slide Mountain, which at 4,180 feet is the tallest of the Catskill peaks, so tall it may have stood above the glacial ice sheets that swept down from the north during the last ice age.

From the top of Slide on a nice day, you can see the mountain escarpment across which the Devil's Path wends its way, the Ashokan Reservoir glittering in the distance, and but for a grove of conifers, you would be able to identify the Shawangunk mountains where I had been standing just the day before and and pick out High Point and Skytop tower.

But today there was no view, just mist. I shambled over to a plaque set into a rock slab, which during prior visits I had never bothered to read. It celebrated the life of John Burroughs, a man about whom I knew nothing at all.

True, I had heard him referred to as the John Muir of the East, but this didn't help much, because I didn't really know anything about Muir either. After the through-run was over, I decided to learn something about Burroughs's life. A naturalist and an essayist of great renown in the late nineteenth and early twentieth centuries, he had grown up on a farm in the Catskills and, after a few years in Washington, D.C., returned to build a house on the shore of the Hudson River just a few miles southeast of Slide Mountain.

Burroughs wrote about the mountains, forests, rivers, people, and wildlife of the Catskills. He was a keen observer of nature, which he recorded with scientific accuracy, but in his essays he tried to bring nature to life by infusing it with the emotions he felt. He struck me as pragmatic and balanced, and while his writing could be incisive, he seemed to have a gentle soul.

I was surprised to discover that Burroughs felt certain reservations about Henry David Thoreau, whom he regarded as more of a mystic than a naturalist. While Burroughs acknowledged Thoreau was a diligent observer of nature, he criticized him for seeing and recording "nothing new." And, while Burroughs praised him for sincerity, he nonetheless regarded Thoreau as a "crusty" person, devoid of compassion, sympathy, pity, generosity, or love. Burroughs wrote that Thoreau "was of the stuff that saints and martyrs and devotees, or, if you please, fanatics are made of and, no doubt, in an earlier age, would have faced the rack or the stake with perfect composure." But having made those points, Burroughs went on to write that "Thoreau's life showed a devotion to principle such as one life in millions does not show; and matching this there runs through his works a vein of the purest and rarest poetry and the finest wisdom."

While living in Washington, D.C., Burroughs met Walt Whitman and over the years became a great friend, admirer, and defender of the controversial poet. Burroughs seemed to respond to a quality of raw vitality in the man. "He reminds one of the first men, the beginners," Burroughs wrote—"has a primitive, outdoor look—not so much from being in the open air as from the texture and quality of his make—a look as of the earth, the sea, or the mountains."

In later years, Burroughs defended Whitman as the "poet of democracy," one who expressed the energy of the new nation, in contrast with those who fixated on tradition, convention, and superficial beauty. What Whitman lacked, according to Burroughs, was the niceties of modern society. "He was a barbarian," Burroughs wrote, "entirely of the open air as opposed to parlors and libraries."

Burroughs is not as widely read today as Thoreau, but during his lifetime his essays were enormously popular and inspired a wave of enthusiasm for conservation. As his fame spread, he was sought out by thousands of visitors, ranging from college students to the rich and famous. He was befriended by Henry Ford, who revered him as a sage and treated him as a hero, providing complimentary cars and drivers and including him on holiday camping trips together with Thomas Edison and Harvey Firestone. They called themselves "the Four Vagabonds," and the younger men were delighted when Burroughs beat them in wood-chopping contests, which he did routinely even at age eighty-three. In 1899, the railroad tycoon E. H. Harriman invited Burroughs to accompany a star-studded expedition to Alaska in the capacity of official historian. On board the steamship, Burroughs befriended Harriman's son, young Averell, future governor of New York, whose mother would one day present a deed and check to the state of New Jersey for the establishment of Harriman State Park. Later, Averell Harriman would commemorate the park's formation by commissioning the statue of Burroughs's friend Walt Whitman, which now stands at Bear Mountain.

Theodore Roosevelt was a great friend and admirer of Burroughs. An accomplished naturalist himself, Roosevelt respected Burroughs's scientific knowledge and loved his essays, which he had first read while traveling in Europe as a young man, and which he wrote had made him feel homesick for the American wilderness. While president, Roosevelt invited Burroughs along on a two-week trip to Yellowstone National Park, in part to promote the importance of conservation, and in part because he enjoyed Burroughs's company (the president took to calling him "Oom John," Dutch for "uncle"). Both men were awestruck by the elk and mountain goats, and they laughed at each other when they fell on their faces in the snow trying to ski. Roosevelt and Burroughs were both passionate about birds. One day at lunch in the White House, the two men fell into a loud debate over the song of what they called the "Chippy Sparrow," unable to agree on whether it chirped two times in a row or three. Another time, the two went hiking in the woods around Washington, D.C., where they observed seventy-five different species of songbird. The day ended in a tie, with each man identifying all but two: the ever-competitive Roosevelt had kept careful score. Roosevelt dedicated one of his books to Burroughs, and in it he wrote that "No bird escaped John Burroughs' eye; no bird note escaped his ear."

"I go to Nature to be soothed and healed," Burroughs wrote, "and to have my senses put in tune once more." An early color film of Burroughs, filmed in 1919, when he was eighty-two years old, shows him sitting at a desk in his barn working on his writing, a tall, thin man with a wide straw hat and a bushy white beard. A trio of young children arrives, and Burroughs takes them exploring in the nearby fields. They admire a chipmunk, a grasshopper, a butterfly. The film is silent, and Burroughs's comments appear in script: "I have reached the summit of my years, but I have the heart of a young man because I have learned to see and appreciate the beauty that is all around us."

Slide Mountain had long intrigued him, and in one of his essays, he described the mountain's distinctive silhouette:

[There is,] amid the group of mountains, one that looks like
the back and shoulders of a gigantic horse. The horse has

got his head down grazing; the shoulders are high, and the descent from them down his neck very steep; if he were to lift up his head, one sees that it would be carried far above all other peaks, and that the noble beast might gaze straight to his peers in the Adirondacks or the White Mountains. But the lowered head never comes up; some spell or enchantment keeps it down there amid the mighty herd; and the high round shoulders and the smooth strong back of the steed are alone visible. The peak to which I refer is Slide Mountain, the highest of the Catskills by some two hundred feet, and probably the most inaccessible; certainly the hardest to get a view of, it is hedged about so completely by other peaks,—the greatest mountain of them all, and apparently the least willing to be seen; only at a distance of thirty or forty miles is it seen to stand up above all other peaks.

I had seen Slide Mountain exactly the way he described it, from the summit of High Point on the Shawangunk Ridge, the day before.

In 1887, at age forty-seven, Burroughs set off to climb Slide Mountain. Together with a trio of local friends, he hiked up a stream to the base of the mountain, camped, and the next day they made their way to the summit. It was slow going, taking nearly seven hours to fight their way seven miles through thick vegetation and over steep ledges to the top. When they finally arrived, they sat down and savored their triumph:

We saw the world as the hawk or the balloonist sees it when he is three thousand feet in the air. How soft and flowing all the outlines of the hills and mountains beneath us looked! The forests dropped down and undulated away over them, covering them like a carpet. . . . All was mountain and forest on every hand. Civilization seemed to have done little more than to have scratched this rough, shaggy surface of the earth here and there. In any such view, the wild, the aboriginal, the geographical greatly predominate. The works of man dwindle, and the original features of the huge globe come out. Every single object or point is dwarfed; the valley of the Hudson is only a wrinkle in the earth's surface. You discover with a feeling of surprise that the great thing is the earth itself, which stretches away on every hand so far beyond your ken.

∼

I climbed down from Slide Mountain on a steep trail. In two places, sturdy wooden ladders had been bolted to the face of the mountain. Then there were scrambles through clefts in the sandstone cliffs. It felt like climbing down a jungle gym.

The trail took me up and over two other summits, Wittenberg and Cornell, but with the overcast sky, there wasn't much point in stopping. A little later, heading down a steep trail toward the valley floor, I passed a forest ranger lugging cans of paint up the mountain to refresh one of the lean-tos. We chatted for a bit about the Catskills's slow, rugged trails. She commented that hikers typically average about one mile per hour. I nodded, but felt that as a runner I was surely moving at a much faster pace.

At the bottom of the mountain, the Long Path turned onto a paved road and proceeded through a deep valley with steep slopes on either side. The small town of Phoenicia was about six miles away. I jogged slowly, took a few walking breaks, and made decent progress—in any case, something faster than one mile per hour.

I was focused, as always, on the road in front of my feet and the next aqua blaze. Had I looked up and to the right, I would have seen a ridgeline descending from the mountain range I had just traversed. I didn't know it at the time, but the Trail Conference had created a committee to oversee the Long Path and appointed two volunteer co-chairs who were busy at work on the top of that ridge, moving boulders, smashing rocks, and carving a new trail into the rough terrain. When finished, this trail would take the Long Path down into the town of Phoenicia through the woods, bypassing the paved road that I was now following.

Who were these people? Later that fall, my son Philip and I would join a volunteer crew working on this new trail and meet the Long Path co-chairs. A strongly built man with a barrel chest, thick spectacles, and a big smile, Andy Garrison struck me as "all teeth and eyes," the way a young Theodore Roosevelt was once described. Andy would say something funny, then stare at you through his thick glasses, a big grin on his face, watching for your reaction. Working on the trail, he swings a heavy sledgehammer with gusto, or uses heavy rock bars to manhandle boulders into place. Jakob Franke is a suave Dutchman with a close-cropped beard. In his seventies, he swings a pickax with an authority that puts younger people to shame.

John Burroughs would have liked these guys. Burroughs was himself a vigorous man, described as having "hands calloused by farm labor" and a face "tanned with wind and sun." When he wasn't writing, entertaining visitors, or wandering, Burroughs gathered crops, chopped and sawed wood, and cleared brush. He built a cabin for himself, including the stone chimney and birch wood furniture. In his late sixties, Burroughs helped his son construct a house, walking nine miles one day to scout out the best lumber, and throwing himself wholeheartedly into the manual labor. "I am always happy," he once wrote in a letter, "digging out rocks and stones to build something with."

When they met me, Andy and Jakob winked at each other, as if to say that running on the trail was no doubt a worthwhile endeavor, but working on a trail crew would teach me what the Long Path was really about.

᙮

Soon enough I arrived in Phoenicia, feeling suddenly triumphant, and made my way straight to Brio's, the town's well-known pizza restaurant. It was late afternoon, and I was a full day behind schedule, but right now that didn't matter. I'd been looking forward to a break in Phoenicia for quite some time, as the town marks mile 186 on the Long Path, a few miles past the halfway mark. Notwithstanding whatever challenges might be lying in wait for me on the second half, a small celebration was in order.

A seat was available on the outdoor patio, where I could enjoy the sunshine and breeze, listen to the chatter of tourists, and discretely remove shoes and socks (not perhaps the proper behavior for a fine restaurant like Brio's, but no one said anything). The pizza and beer were perfect. I settled back in the chair, content and at peace with the world.

Mindful of the need for calories, and conscious that I had been prioritizing time over sustenance, I ordered a chocolate milkshake for desert. By the time it went down, I had eaten so much I felt positively ill.

Having paid the bill, I waddled down the street in search of an outfitter, looking for a warm shirt and hat. It had been chilly at night, and the Long Path would take me back up above three thousand feet in elevation for the next two nights. The town's gas station provided some extra blister supplies (just in case), fresh batteries, and a chocolate bar.

By now a couple of hours had slipped by in Phoenicia, and the clock was still ticking. Sadly, it was time to move on.

Still digesting the large meal, I shuffled along the road out of town, looking for the turnoff onto a narrow footpath heading uphill. Five days ago, I had driven back and forth on this road, staring through the windshield at blazes painted on the trees, struggling to locate the path. It was just like the trailhead on Berme Road: the Long Path disks were nailed to trees just a few yards off the road, making it difficult to spot from the car. One day I'd have to ask Andy and Jakob why it was so hard to find the Long Path. Were they just being discrete? I imagined Andy looking at me through his glasses, a grin on his face, asking, was I just being blind? Maybe it was just as well. For the trail now led straight to the Devil's Path, and perhaps it was better not to encourage casual visitors to the Devil's refuge.

A hundred yards up the trail, I turned off to the right and after a minute or two retrieved my fourth drop bag. Having eaten as much as my stomach would hold, and now having resupplied, I was ready for the next leg. And that was a good thing, because the next fifty miles would traverse nine separate peaks, including four along the Devil's Path and then Blackhead Mountain, one of the tallest in the Catskills, notorious for a steep scramble at the summit.

For now, I felt great. Fueled by pizza, beer, and chocolate shake, I practically shot up the trail, even though it was steep, eroded, and strewn with large rocks. This is typical for logging roads, which were built to extract timber quickly and cheaply and typically constructed without the water bars, culverts, or switchbacks necessary to prevent erosion. On these roads, rainfall strips away the dirt, leaving a washed-out surface of gravel and rock.

The late afternoon continued pleasantly warm and sunny. Maple and beech grew on the steep slope and towered overhead. The forest seemed immense.

After a thousand-foot climb, the trail leveled off. Dusk began to fall, and I started to jog, determined to get as far as possible while the light lasted. No matter how bright my flashlight, progress at night would be slower. A few minutes later I arrived at the summit of Mount Tremper, where an old fire tower reaches to the sky. I took a few steps up the rickety stairs and thought better of it. In the remaining light, I headed down the far side of the mountain, running easily on a smooth downhill trail, excited to be moving quickly for a change.

The trail led down to a stream crossing deep in the bowels of the mountains. It was dark, quiet, and isolated. The path hopped across the stream on a series of rocks and then followed a logging road, which was blazed with reflective disks that glinted in the beam of the flashlight from a long ways off. That is, until I looked up and saw the glints were gone. Out came the course notes—and how could this be a surprise—they indicated a turnoff from the logging road onto a footpath. I couldn't tell if I had missed the turnoff, or whether it still lay in front. Accordingly, I backtracked, found the blazes again, then turned around and moved forward, this time counting my steps to track the distance. Again the blazes ended with no sign of a turnoff. Again, I retraced my steps (meaning to be triple sure), and then, taking a deep breath, I plunged forward on the logging road and into the unknown, fearful that I would meander off course and become hopelessly lost at night, in the middle of nowhere. But there was a glint of light, and the blazes resumed. I followed them onto the turnoff and up a steep trail.

The slope was moderate and the footing wasn't bad. But in the darkness, there were no landmarks, no way to gauge progress. Time went by slowly. Eventually the trail reached a saddle on the ridge, where the Long Path joined up with the Devil's Path, blazed with red disks, which seemed an appropriate color. My destination for this evening was a lean-to about five miles ahead, which meant as much as two or even three more hours. I walked along at a steady pace, alone in the darkness, conscious of nothing but the dim shapes of trees, the texture of the path under foot, and the slow passage of time.

The path went up and over Plateau Mountain. The trail was well marked and easy to follow, but I referred constantly to the notes, wanting to know my exact location at every point in time, desperate for some indication of progress. I kept jumping ahead in the notes, thinking I had already arrived at the summit, but if that was so, why was the trail still heading uphill?

Somehow I finally made it to the summit and then down the back side of Plateau Mountain. At the next intersection, there was a sign pointing to my destination, the Mink Hollow Lean-To, just a tenth of mile to the right. I wandered down the trail, playing my light through the trees, but no structure was visible. I returned to the intersection and tried again, this time counting steps. The trail headed further downhill and became rocky. After what seemed like an endless trek, the lean-to finally appeared. Never had a tenth of a mile seemed so long.

The lean-to was beautiful: clean, spacious, freshly painted, and empty. It might have been a luxury resort. Unbuckling my gear, I lay down on the hard wooden surface.

Today's efforts had yielded another thirty-five miles. It had been long and steep, taking me over five mountain summits: Slide, Cornell, Wittenberg, Tremper, and Plateau. Those mountains plus the break in Phoenicia might explain why my average pace had slowed to an unimpressive one-and-a-half miles per hour.

Today's journey had also brought me to the two-hundred-mile mark—but it was better not to think about this. More sensible to stay focused. Survive the Catskills. Get out of these rugged, rocky mountains. Get off this steep, twisted trail.

Another forty miles through the Catskills, and things would have to get easier. Surely there would be a length of reasonable trail, one that wasn't rocky, steep, overgrown, or blockaded with downed trees. A section of trail where I could stretch out my legs and *run*! Make up some time. Knock off some distance. Maybe start to think about getting this adventure over and done with.

Forty miles to go, and I'd escape from the Catskills. I'd be practically home free.

The forest was silent, but for an occasional drop of water falling from a leaf. I listened for a little bit, until the drops ceased.

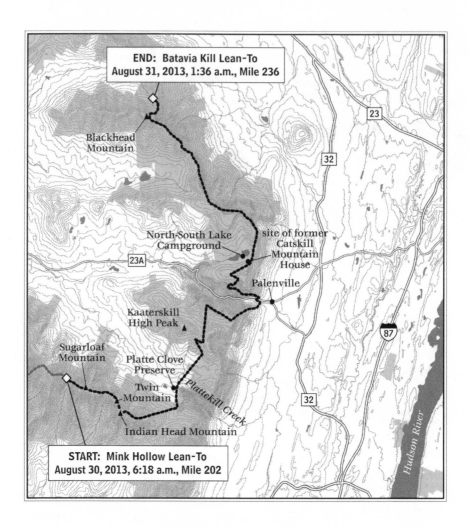

END: Batavia Kill Lean-To
August 31, 2013, 1:36 a.m., Mile 236

Blackhead
Mountain

North-South Lake
Campground

site of former
Catskill
Mountain
House

Palenville

Kaaterskill
High Peak

Sugarloaf
Mountain

Platte Clove
Preserve

Twin
Mountain

Plattekill Creek

Indian Head Mountain

START: Mink Hollow Lean-To
August 30, 2013, 6:18 a.m., Mile 202

Hudson River

Chapter 8

Escape from the Catskills

I inhale great draughts of space,
The east and the west are mine, and the north and the south
  are mine.

—Walt Whitman, "Song of the Open Road"

These mountains we behold and cross are not picturesque,—they are wild and inhuman as the sea. In them you are in a maze, in a weltering world of woods; you can see neither the earth nor the sky, but a confusion of the growth and decay of centuries.

—John Burroughs, *Locusts and Wild Honey*

Mink Hollow Lean-To, Friday, August 30, 6:18 a.m.

I woke up at first light.

I wasn't eager to face the Devil's Path. Not only because of the incessant climbing, but because my water was running low, and so was my food. Between the lean-to and my next drop bag stood at least six mountains, including Blackhead Mountain, whose summit is particularly treacherous.

I pulled the poncho liner over my head and went back to sleep.

Thirty minutes later I woke up again, and this time was able to sit up, suit up, and eventually get going. Leaving the lean-to, I rejoined the Devil's Path and took on the morning's first challenge, Sugar Loaf Mountain. From a distance, the mountain looks just like a loaf of bread, and you might think the slope would be mellow. But looks can be deceiving. The path was an almost continuous scramble, from one rock ledge to the next. You have to grab tree branches or roots to hoist yourself up over each rock face, and then after the briefest section of level trail, you encounter another scramble.

Somewhere near the top, I paused to admire the view from a stone ledge that jutted out into space. The morning sun was shining on the far side of a steep valley. I leaned my trekking poles against a fir tree and pulled out my camera. This was the kind of spot where you imagine an eagle would build its nest. Burroughs had written about the eagle's view: "[The eagle] draws great lines across the sky; he sees the forests like a carpet beneath him; he sees the hills and valleys as folds and wrinkles in a many-colored tapestry; he sees the river as a silver belt connecting remote horizons. We climb mountain-peaks to get a glimpse of the spectacle that is hourly spread out beneath him. Dignity, elevation, repose are his. I would have my thoughts take as wide a sweep. I would be as far removed from the petty cares and turmoils of this noisy and blustering world."

From this vantage, I scrambled down a series of rock ledges and arrived at the saddle between Sugar Loaf and Twin Mountains. I paused to pull out my trekking poles for the next uphill climb—and discovered they were missing. To retrieve them or to abandon them, was the question. With a sigh, I faced about, scrambled back up to the eagle's nest, and found the poles leaning against the tree, just where I had left them.

Twin Mountain was next. I scrambled up and over the west peak, enjoying the views from breaks in the trees, and then scrambled up and over the east peak.

Indian Head was more of the same. At three thousand feet the air was cool, the sun was bright, the views were expansive, and the scrambles weren't as taxing as I had feared. I no longer stopped at each vantage point, but as I moved along the trail I was conscious of light, air, space, and great distance, as well as the fragrance of the fir and spruce trees.

The forest on either side of the path was dark, the floor covered with brown needles and strewn with dead branches.

The tops of these mountains are cloaked in red spruce and Balsam fir, Christmas tree–like conifers growing from ten to twenty-five feet tall, remnants of the boreal forests that have largely retreated from the Hudson Valley to far northern climates. Deciduous trees such as beech, birch, and maple grow taller and live longer than the spruce and fir, depriving the shorter conifers of light. As the glaciers retreated and the climate became milder, these hardwoods first invaded the valleys and then moved up the ridges, displacing the spruce and fir wherever the soil was deep enough to support their roots. But on the Catskills' high ledges and summits, where the soil is thin, the hardwoods cannot hold on. They get knocked down by heavy snow, thick ice, and fierce winds, which the tough little conifers survive. Hikers bushwhacking across the Catskills encounter impenetrable jungles of spruce and fir, growing tightly together with branches intertwined, creating a joint defense against the elements, like a phalanx of ancient soldiers locking their shields together.

The Balsam fir is also distinctive because of the resinous blisters covering the trunks and branches. The Indians of New York called the tree *Cho-koh-tung*, or "blister," and believed the resin helped heal infected wounds and cancerous growths. Hearing from the Indians of the tree's powers, eighteenth-century Europeans thought it must be the source of the healing balm the Israelites had found on Mount Gilead (Jeremiah 8:22). Europeans named it the "balm of Gilead tree" and dispatched traders into the forests to harvest seeds, with plans to grow and sell the tree in England. This was a surprisingly difficult endeavor, because the seeds are covered in sticky resin until they mature in September, at which point the cones quickly disintegrate, scattering the seeds to the winds and the animals. When seeds were finally collected, the Balsam fir did not thrive on British soil, and European interest waned.

After Indian Head Mountain, the Long Path separated from the Devil's Path and ran downhill into Platte Clove Wilderness Preserve, a private nature preserve. I had brought the family here once on a camping trip, and a memory popped into my mind of a younger version of myself, wearing boots and carrying a rucksack with tent, stove, and sleeping bag—totally different from my current kit—yet back then I couldn't help but trot down the trail, hopping from rock to rock, a spring in my step, a smile on my face. With that kind of attitude, it was no surprise that I had eventually discovered trail running. This morning, there was a little less spring in my step, what with two hundred miles under the belt. But it felt great to be off the Devil's Path and heading downhill. And being quite thirsty again, I was looking forward to the large stream at the base of the hill.

And I wasn't disappointed: the Plattekill was rushing cold and clear, tumbling over black rocks, passing under a wooden footbridge that led out of the preserve. Settling down on the bank, I fished a thirty-two-ounce plastic bag from my pack, dipped it into the stream until it was full, then screwed on a lightweight water filter and gulped the cold, clear water directly from the nozzle. Then I filtered more water and drank again. My thirst finally slaked, I refilled the camelback and rehydrated a package of freeze-dried pad thai noodles. I let the meal have a few minutes to soften and then attacked it, crunching through noodles there were still rock-hard, spooning out the other, largely unidentifiable ingredients, and then tilting the package back and draining the last drop of broth. It didn't taste much like the pad thai they serve you in restaurants, but it was good enough.

Refreshed, refueled, and suddenly in really good spirits, I strode across the wooden bridge and then crossed a narrow paved road, which descends through a steep gorge to the plains of the Hudson Valley fourteen hundred feet below. At the top of the gorge, the sandstone has fractured along vertical joints, and the gorge is essentially a rockslide full of boulders that have split off and tumbled down between precipitous walls. The Plattekill Creek plunges downward through this gorge and reportedly traverses seventeen waterfalls on the way down, some as high as seventy feet. At the bottom of the gorge, cool water collects in crystal pools surrounded by lush vegetation. There are dangerous, unmarked trails that wind up along the falls. The paved road, which hugs the far side of the gorge, is open only during the summer. Fortunately, I would not be heading in this direction.

Instead, the path headed across the road and into a small parking area at the foot of the next challenge, a twelve-hundred-foot climb up and over the shoulder of Kaaterskill High Peak. This spot brought back memories. It was here that I had dropped out of Manitou's Revenge, the early June race that was supposed to be a training run and confidence-builder. I recalled how, after twelve hours struggling over steep climbs and rough trails, I had arrived at this parking lot in low spirits. The path across Kaaterskill was heavily eroded, with rocks and roots sticking out of pools of muddy black water. Having started the race in a weak condition, I had stumbled across this part of the trail, unable to run, barely able to walk, frustrated to the point of tears. The only positive was the aid station set up in the parking lot. Staffed with friendly volunteers, there was a large supply of watermelon, which I fell onto with great gusto, and soon felt substantially better. But for me, the race was over. A volunteer named Cal Johnson drove me back to Phoenicia.

Today I felt better, and having just eaten and drunk my fill, I glanced dismissively at the steep climb, dug in with the poles (retrieving them was indeed the right decision), and went to work. Breathing heavily, I marched uphill, passing a side trail to a vantage point. But I didn't have time to sightsee. The trail at the top was swampy and difficult, but not quite as wet as I recalled from Manitou's Revenge, and I managed to keep moving at a brisk pace.

On the far side of Kaaterskill High Peak, the trail followed a long shelf, passing by two pretty waterfalls that overlook the Kaaterskill Clove. In 1823, an Englishman named Thomas Cole had taken a steamer up the Hudson, and on a whim had gone hiking in this general area. Enchanted by the show of autumnal color, Cole fell in love with the Catskills. His paintings, detailed and realistic yet also romantic, were enormously influential in the mid-nineteenth century, and Cole is credited as the founder of a movement that came to be known as the Hudson River School. Cole painted a number of famous images in this area, including the Kaaterskill waterfall and the Catskill Mountain House, both situated across the valley to the north.

Cole believed that a landscape painter needed to observe nature firsthand. He ranged through the Catskills during the summer, braving the terrain and weather, making detailed sketches of lakes, rock formations, and vegetation, and taking notes on the colors he observed. From these sketches and notes, he created oil paintings during the winter in a studio in the small town of Catskill on the Hudson River, where he married and settled down. From his house, it was a fifteen-mile hike to the lower slopes of the Catskills. From his desk on the second floor or a seat on the front porch, you can see the mountains silhouetted against the sky.

Similar to nineteenth-century European artists, Cole sought out the picturesque, sublime, and magnificent. But the European landscape tradition portrayed nature in the context of antiquity and cultivation. In American scenery, Cole saw nature in its primeval state. "The most distinctive, and perhaps most impressive, characteristic of American scenery," he wrote, "is its wildness."

Through his paintings, Cole created romantic images of an untouched wilderness, and his work came to symbolize the seemingly unspoiled character of a new nation. He hoped that as Americans admired the beauty of the wild, they would contemplate freedom, goodness, and the hand of the Creator.

One of his most famous paintings, *A View of the Two Lakes and Mountain House, Catskill Mountains, Morning*, hangs on the fifth floor of the Brooklyn Museum, just down the hall from a famous painting of George Washington. On Cole's canvas, you can see the small figures of tourists staying at the Catskill Mountain House, the premier resort hotel of the early nineteenth century. These tourists had been awakened early so that they could admire the sun rising over the Hudson Valley. And perhaps, as Cole hoped, the view inspired in them an appreciation of freedom, goodness, and God.

But it's one thing to watch the sun rise from the comfort of a first-class hotel. It's altogether different when you stand on that ledge having climbed a thousand feet up on a rocky trail. You brush the sweat from your face as you scan the rolling mountains and valley floor spreading out toward the horizon, and discover that you have crossed a vast landscape—and now you understand that the energy of life can be measured in terms of distance and time.

∿

From the shoulder of Kaaterskill, there was a steep trail leading down 1,500 feet to the valley floor. I trotted downhill at a steady pace, quads absorbing the shock of each step. Three young girls out for a hike smiled and waved as they headed uphill.

The trail bottomed out on the valley floor and turned left onto a quiet tree-lined street in the tiny town of Palenville. A large Victorian house stood to the left of the road. A sign read "Fernwood." Odd for a house to have a name, I thought to myself, wondering whether this might be a restaurant. Sure enough, Visa and MasterCard decals graced the door. I hobbled up onto a broad porch. Opening time was 5:00 p.m., according to a placard. To my chagrin, my watch showed 4:00 p.m. I stared wistfully through the window, making out a long bar and round tables in a large, empty room. Hoping against all hope, I rattled the knob, but the door was locked. Just as I was turning on my heel to go, the door slammed open, and a stout Labrador rushed out and ran around in circles on the deck barking furiously. A second later a man emerged, collared the dog, and then introduced himself as Emil, the proprietor.

When he heard my story, Emil brought me a glass of Coke and refused to take any cash. Then he brought me a second glass. The cold drink was refreshing and gave me new energy. I toyed with the idea of staying for dinner, but with the clock ticking, it was time to move on. I vowed to return with the family for a celebratory dinner, should my quest prove successful.

The Long Path continued down the quiet, tree-lined street until it reached a barricade, then passed onto an abandoned road, asphalt cracked and broken. Emerging onto a bridge, the path ran along the shoulder of a two-lane road for a short distance, then entered a parking area. This was the base of the Kaaterskill Clove, another deep gorge in the mountain rampart above the Hudson River Valley. The path would now take me back up into the heights. If all went well, sometime later this evening, I would be crossing Blackhead Mountain, three thousand feet above my current elevation.

I rustled through my pack looking for food. There was one freeze-dried meal left. Better save that for dinner, which I'd eat at North-South Lake Campground, a thousand feet higher up. Instead, I gobbled up a large bar of dark chocolate, which seemed to get the motor going again, and headed up a rocky dirt road at a brisk hike, feeling energetic and relaxed, and enjoying the late afternoon sunlight.

It was somewhere in this gorge, I reflected, that Rip Van Winkle and his dog Wolf had encountered the ghosts of Henry Hudson's crew playing a game of nine-pins. After drinking the spirits' liquor, Rip laid down for a brief rest and woke up twenty years later. This story was all many people knew about the Catskills, and over the years, Rip Van Winkle had become the area's unofficial mascot and guardian spirit. In 1966, developers came up with the Disneyesque idea of building a three-thousand-seat amphitheater, where each summer a musical based on the legend would be shown. The complex would also include shops and restaurants. However, the developers were unsuccessful in raising capital for the project.

After an hour or so, the trail reached an open field on a ledge high above the valley with views back toward Kaaterskill High Peak and out across the Hudson Valley, the river itself visible as a ribbon of silver in the distance. This was the site of the former Catskill Mountain House, the famous hotel that Cole had painted in 1844. Built in 1823, it was considered American's "first resort," and at its height was patronized by the rich and famous, including such luminaries as President Theodore Roosevelt. For a few years, the hotel even had its own railroad to carry visitors up from the Hudson, sparing them a bone-jolting carriage ride. (The train did not prove economic and ended up sold for scrap.)

Over time, the Catskills were eclipsed by the Adirondacks and then other destinations for wealthy travelers. Middle-class tourists found the hotel expensive and opted instead for bungalows or campgrounds. The Catskill Mountain House closed after its last season in 1941. In 1963, the state deemed it a hazard and an eyesore and burned it to the ground. From America's first resort to an empty field, this was another example of the "confusion of growth and decay," the phrase that Burroughs had used to describe the tangled Catskill forests, but that often applies just as well to human activity.

Around the corner from the former hotel was its successor, North-South Lake Campground, which included a roped-off beach, showers and washrooms, picnic tables, open grills, campsites, and a parking lot. On a typical summer afternoon, there would be crowds of people splashing in the water, lounging on the sand, barbequing on the grills, enjoying the beautiful views, tossing Frisbees, playing loud music, laughing.

But today, to my disappointment, the campground was deserted. Where was everybody? Wasn't this a holiday weekend? I struggled to recall what day of the week it was.

I had joked about the Long Path as a parallel universe, which in contrast to the attributes of modern life, is small, quiet, slow, and empty. But now, as I surveyed the vacant parking lot, it seemed a little too empty.

Maybe there really were people here, I thought. Maybe I had journeyed so far into this parallel universe that real people were no longer visible to me, nor I to them.

I wandered over to a small playground, found a picnic table, and plopped down onto the bench. There were people here: three little kids frolicking on the swings and a dad sitting on the side, swatting at mosquitoes, looking bored and miserable. From time to time he would beg them to finish up. The kids ignored him for a while. Eventually they left.

Now completely alone, I sat at the picnic table and worked my way through a rehydrated camping meal. It wasn't very appetizing, but

I needed the calories, and this would be my last meal until Route 23. There would be no breakfast tomorrow.

It was time to go. The path led me out of the campground and uphill, past several rock ledges with breathtaking views, including Artist's Ledge and then North Point. To the right was Kaaterskill High Peak and behind it, the Devil's Path. To the left, open plains stretched out toward the Hudson River. Here and there lights twinkled out in the valley, but the landscape seemed largely empty. A breeze picked up and tall yellow grass waved in the twilight.

Cole had visited this spot on many occasions to sketch the lakes, the Mountain House, and the distant mountains. He was enthralled by these mountains, yet he worried that the masses cared little for natural beauty, that the pressure for improvement would leave the forests axed, the landscape desecrated. "We are still in Eden," he once wrote. "The wall that shuts us out of the garden is our own ignorance and folly."

❧

As the dusk deepened, I listened for the song of the hermit thrush, which I had heard during previous journeys into the mountains. Its song consists of an initial whistle, followed by two or three softer, descending, echo-like tones. The bird repeats the song, but alternates the key. People describe it as ethereal, flute-like, and haunting, and some consider it North America's most beautiful bird song.

In the summer of 1865, John Burroughs spent a few vacation weeks back at home in the Catskills. While out for a hike, he heard the hermit thrush singing near Batavia Mountain. On returning to his job in Washington, D.C., he reported this discovery with great excitement to Walt Whitman, his friend and mentor. Burroughs described the song as "clear, flutelike, deliberate," an evening hymn, a voice of "calm, sweet solemnity," and suggested Whitman work the hermit thrush song into the eulogy for Abraham Lincoln that he was then writing.

"Sings oftener after sundown . . . is very secluded . . . likes shaded, dark places," Whitman noted in his diary. "His song is a hymn . . . in swamps—is very shy . . . never sings near the farm houses—never in the settlement—is the bird of the solemn primal woods & of Nature pure & holy."

Whitman's eulogy, "When Lilacs Last in the Dooryard Bloom'd," never mentions Lincoln by title or name. It is considered the most important of his collection of Civil War poems, *Drum Taps*.

> When lilacs last in the dooryard bloom'd,
> And the great star early droop'd in the western sky in the
>   night,
> I mourn'd, and yet shall mourn with ever-returning spring.
> . . .
> In the swamp, in secluded recesses,
> A shy and hidden bird is warbling a song.
> Solitary, the thrush,
> The hermit, withdrawn to himself, avoiding the settlements,
> Sings by himself a song.
> Song of a bleeding throat . . .
> . . . .
> Sing on, sing on, you gray-brown bird,
> Sing from the swamps, the recesses, pour your chant from
>   the bushes,
> Limitless out of the dusk, out of the cedars and pines.
> Sing on, dearest brother, warble your reedy song,
> Loud human song, with voice of uttermost woe.
> . . .
> Then with the knowledge of death as walking one side of me,
> And the thought of death close-walking the other side of me,
> And I in the middle as with companions, and as holding the
>   hands of companions,
> I fled forth to the hiding receiving night that talks not,

Down to the shores of the water, the path by the swamp in
the dimness,
To the solemn shadowy cedars and ghostly pines so still.

And the singer so shy to the rest receiv'd me,
The gray-brown bird I know receiv'd us comrades three,
And he sang the carol of death, and a verse for him I love.

From deep secluded recesses,
From the fragrant cedars and the ghostly pines so still,
Came the carol of the bird.

When I read the poem, I tried to imagine what it would have been like to live through the assassination of Abraham Lincoln. Tried to picture the "Coffin that passes through lanes and streets / Through day and night with the great cloud darkening the land."

Whitman had spent the war years in the hospitals of Washington, D.C., caring for wounded soldiers, some of whom died in his arms. He believed in the Union, which Lincoln had saved, and he understood the human cost.

That evening I listened for the thrush, but didn't hear it.

Now in darkness, I moved along the ridge, occasionally glimpsing lights in the distance. They might have been the lights of Albany, or of small towns in the Hudson Valley. I didn't stop to look, but as I passed I was conscious of space and distance.

The trail rose along the ridge and soon reached a peak called Estoppel Point, where my flashlight played over the wreckage of a single-engine airplane that had crashed here many years ago. I had been here several times before, and each time the crash site came into view, I marveled that a plane could have landed intact in the thick forest of a mountain slope, and I wondered if the pilot had survived.

This section of the Long Path coincides with the Escarpment Trail, along which the Escarpment Trail Run is held each year on the last weekend in July. The race organizer warns would-be participants that the trail "is viewed by many as an exaggeration of the term. It is extremely rocky and a runner must expect to navigate over boulders, downed trees, gullies and hidden roots the entire distance." The website shows the picture of the 2010 and 2011 female winner Kristen Tamburrino, blood oozing from her knee and running down her shin.

But compared to the Devil's Path, Kaatterskill High Peak, or the ascent of Peekamoose, I found the Escarpment Trail to be well-marked and impeccably maintained. Later on I would learn that Cal Johnson, the same person who had driven me back to the start when I dropped out of Manitou's Revenge, was the volunteer supervisor for this section of the trail. As supervisor, he oversaw a crew of volunteer "maintainers," each responsible for a mile or two of the trail. Along the Escarpment Trail, he would explain to me, one of the biggest challenges was pruning back the blackberry vines that, if left unchecked, would choke off the path. Cal equipped his maintainers with heavy-duty shears with long handles, implements that could reach past the thorns to cut the offending vines at their roots, but were heavy and difficult to manipulate. If the maintainers didn't get the job done to his satisfaction, he'd go out there and finish the work himself. Well, the attention to detail showed. I walked briskly and confidently along the trail, even though it was now pitch black.

Moving along the high ridgeline, conscious of lights flashing in the distance, I started for the first time to think about finishing this adventure. I imagined arriving at the finish line in the John Boyd Thacher State Park, crowds cheering and a band playing upbeat tunes. I'd sprint across the finish, a big smile on my face; then, leaning nonchalantly on my trekking poles, I'd regale the crowd with stories and crack a few jokes. Of course, I knew there probably wouldn't be anyone there—and certainly no band. But sometimes indulging in a harmless fantasy can put an extra spring in your step.

Fantasy or not, I was almost done with the Catskills, practically on my way out. True, Blackhead Mountain still lay in wait for me. Glancing at the notes, I saw there was an eight-hundred-foot climb to a grassy plateau called the Arizona Flats (where this name came from was not indicated)—and then another eight-hundred-foot climb to the summit. Another half of a chocolate bar went down the hatch, and I marched forward resolutely.

On the way to the summit, the trail got steeper, and there were a couple of ledges to scramble up, but I recognized these places from the Escarpment Trail Run. The familiar spots made me feel confident and in control. At the summit, more lights were blinking in the distance, and the scramble down from Blackhead, while just as steep as I remembered it, turned out to be anticlimactic. Clicking on my headlamp and stowing the poles in my pack, I availed myself of roots, trees, and handholds on the rock face and lowered myself down without incident.

Past Blackhead, the trail reached an intersection, and the Batavia Kill Lean-To was waiting for me, right where the notes indicated, clean, unoccupied, and welcoming.

Making it to this lean-to felt like a huge accomplishment, and it was. I had banged out another thirty-five miles in the Catskills, bringing me to 240 miles. Another nine miles tomorrow morning would carry me to Route 23, where my fifth drop bag would be waiting. And from there, only 101 miles would remain.

Call it an even hundred miles. Why, I had run that distance before in under twenty-four hours.

True, the next hundred miles of the Long Path had a questionable reputation. Mention the northern sections of the Long Path, and people would say, with a doubtful tone in their voice, "Oh, you know, it's a little overgrown." Dave O'Neill had cautioned me about this. There were comments posted on the Trail Conference's website warning of rough conditions. People had reported problems following the blazes.

But the next hundred miles, no matter how overgrown they might be, couldn't be as rocky as the Catskills. They couldn't be as steep. They couldn't be as slow.

I lay down on the hard wooden floor of the lean-to and covered myself with the poncho liner. One moment, the wind was rushing through the tree tops, sounding like a distant train. The next moment, it was quiet. To my tired mind, the wind sounded mournful, yet it also conveyed a sense of anticipation. Winds of change, I thought to myself sleepily. Autumn comes early to these mountains. The weather could change tomorrow. One must keep moving. Time waits for no man.

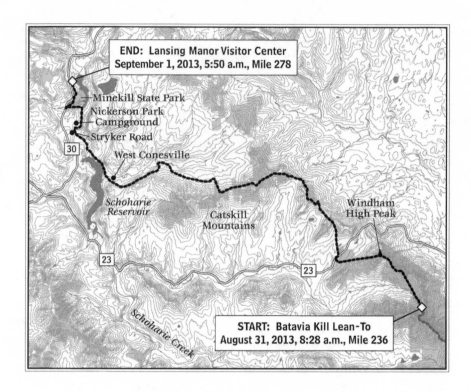

END: Lansing Manor Visitor Center
September 1, 2013, 5:50 a.m., Mile 278

Minekill State Park
Nickerson Park
Campground
Stryker Road
West Conesville

Schoharie
Reservoir

Catskill
Mountains

Windham
High Peak

Schoharie Creek

START: Batavia Kill Lean-To
August 31, 2013, 8:28 a.m., Mile 236

Chapter 9

Northward into Uncharted Realms

From this hour I ordain myself loos'd of limits and imaginary lines,
Going where I list, my own master total and absolute,
Listening to others, considering well what they say,
Pausing, searching, receiving, contemplating,
Gently, but with undeniable will, divesting myself of the holds that
  would hold me.

—Walt Whitman, "Song of the Open Road"

An unknown road is always a long road. We cannot cast the mental
eye along it and see the end from the beginning. We are fighting in
the dark, and cannot take the measure of our foe.

—John Burroughs, *Winter Sunshine*

Batavia Kill Lean-To, Saturday, August 31, 2013, 8:28 a.m.

I woke up in the Batavia Kill Lean-To at first light, but didn't exactly hop
out of bed. Rather, I went back to sleep.

An hour later, I woke up again, but there was to be no breakfast
this morning. The only food left was half a chocolate bar. I closed my
eyes once more.

Another thirty minutes went by before I finally sat up, dragged
myself to my feet, and loaded up. The only thought was to make it nine
miles to Route 23, locate the fifth drop bag, and eat breakfast. The wild

northern sections of the Long Path would be dealt with later. For now, the first step was back uphill to the Escarpment Trail and then off along the spine of the ridge. There were only nine miles to go, but there was at least one mountain peak along the way and two smaller summits. Nine miles could take three hours, or it could take much longer. To conserve energy, I walked, but I tried to walk quickly.

For a change, there were other people on the trail. A couple stood at a vantage point admiring the misty vista. A trio of trail runners passed by heading uphill. Windham High Peak took a long time to reach, but eventually there came into view the large boulder which marks the top and which I recognized as the site of the first-aid station at the Escarpment Trail Run. On the way down from Windham, the trail passed through a forest of Norway spruce and red pine. The great trees soared above and their roots twisted across the path, making for difficult footing.

The nine miles passed slowly but uneventfully, and by late morning I arrived at Route 23 and crossed the road to the parking lot on the far side. This was a familiar spot. It's the starting point for the Escarpment Trail Run. Also, I had come out here once for a training run heading north. And six days ago I had swung by to cache food and water.

Mercifully, the food and water were still behind the old stone wall, right where I had stashed them. Breakfast consisted of a rehydrated camping meal, some slices of dried mango, and a handful of almonds. The Trail Conference notes had warned of brambles on the next section of the trail, and accordingly, I had packed zip-on pant legs in the drop bag. Now I pulled them out and zipped them onto my shorts.

Getting through the Catskills was a major achievement, but with a hundred miles still to go, it was premature to declare victory. A couple of sections of the trail in these parts were familiar to me, but the rest was a great mystery, uncharted territory, the blank spot in the middle of the map that had so intrigued me. Regarding food, there was only one place to stock up, so far as I knew—the small town of Middleburgh, some fifty miles away. If I didn't make it there tonight, I'd run short again. And it was already late morning.

During the nine-mile hike from Batavia Kill Lean-To, I hadn't felt especially hungry. That is to say, my stomach wasn't growling, and I wasn't craving favorite foods. But I could sense that my reserves were running low.

Whatever might happen as the day went on, for now I was refueled, rehydrated, and ready to go. I replaced the drop bag in its hiding spot, piled on a few rocks for extra security, and headed back out onto the trail. The path took me through a forest, then crossed a paved road, headed up a long dirt road, and passed through two gates. I had been out here once before, but little seemed familiar now.

After the second gate, the slope became very steep. And now, for the first time, I noticed that my left ankle was stiff. The inside of my left calf felt tender, too. Something must have gotten strained while scrambling through the Catskills. It wasn't a major problem, just a consideration to be mindful of, especially heading uphill. Marshall Ulrich had run across the United States with tendinitis in his foot. Jennifer Pharr-Davis had put up with shin splints on the Appalachian Trail. Scott Jurek had won ultramarathons with twisted ankles, torn tendons, and a broken toe. If they could manage through aches and pains, then so could I.

The path soon gained the ridgeline and meandered along it for a little ways, heading up one moment, down the next. I gave up trying to follow along in the notes and just hoped for the best. Tall grass grew in many sections of the trail, and in some spots it was hard to see where my feet were landing, making it difficult to run. In other places, brambles tugged at my pants legs as I trudged by. After a little while, the trail opened up into a narrow logging road and I picked up the pace, trotting downhill at a nice clip. But after a minute or so, I looked up and saw that the blazes had vanished. With a sigh, I turned around and retraced my steps back up the hill until I found the path again.

Pausing for a moment, I glanced down at my feet and was surprised to see a stone plaque set in the ground. The memorial was for Donald Sutton, who the plaque said had "hunted these hills for forty years." This reminded me of something John Burroughs had once written: "To learn something new, take the path you took yesterday." Whoever he was, Mr. Sutton must have gotten to know the local paths quite well. Perhaps, like Raymond Torrey, he was a "disciple" of the long brown path.

Later that fall, I returned to this section of the Long Path to revisit the course. I headed back up into the hills, feeling exhilarated to be on the trail again. With the leaves down, the area's topography was now apparent. After crossing Route 23, the Long Path heads up a two-thousand-foot peak, traverses a ridgeline and saddle and summits a second peak, and then descends to the valley floor. With the leaves down, the broad flood plain of the Catskill Creek was visible to the northeast. Fields and hills stretched out toward Albany and the Hudson River, dotted with farmhouses and barns. To the southwest, a small mountain lake sat at the foot of the mountain, and in the distance the Catskills undulated in shades of dark blue. I kept my eyes out for the Sutton memorial, but this time I missed it. Back at home, I searched the Internet, but could find no reference to Donald Sutton. His life remains a mystery to me.

I kept moving. The trail passed through a low-lying forest, ranged over more hills, and crossed a swampy area overgrown with grass, reeds, and brambles. Shoes and socks were once again soaked. Then there was a steep downhill through another stand of Norway spruce and red pine. With the sky overcast and the air full of mist, it was dark and hushed under these trees, and the path was carpeted with their needles.

On my left, a porcupine was climbing a tree. The animal paused on the trunk, looking much like a telephone repairman halfway up a pole, and eyed me suspiciously, as if questioning my right to proceed on the Long Path. Did I not understand that the path belongs to the animals?

Many years ago, Sue and I had joined a hike organized by a local chapter of the Sierra Club. We tramped through the northern Shawangunks for a few hours, then broke for lunch, sitting in a circle and admiring the "million-dollar view" in the distance. I nonchalantly tossed an orange peel in the bushes (after all, it was biodegradable), but I was swiftly scolded by one of our new friends, who warned me that the accumulation of trash could have an impact on the flora and fauna. Gesturing at the view, he warned that a little bit of trash, even an orange peel, could attract porcupines from the Catskills. I snorted to myself in disbelief.

But as time went by, I did indeed begin to notice more porcupines in the Shawangunks. Possibly the orange peel had triggered a mass migration after all, or perhaps I was just spending more time outdoors. Whatever the reason, I'd see them waddling down the trail or draped across a tree branch placidly admiring the views. They struck me as jolly little animals, with little to worry about. Why should they worry? Their quills protect them from all but the fiercest predators. Odie had snapped at one once, and that had cost him a trip to the vet. (No fool, Odie never did that again.)

But this porcupine didn't look jolly, it looked cross, as if it resented my presence in its neighborhood. The porcupine glared at me for another moment, then shimmied down the tree and shuffled off into the bushes.

I returned my attention to the dirt and rocks in front of me, and now I began to notice large frogs sitting on the trail. Unlike their small cousins in the glacial valley in Harriman, these frogs didn't seem scared, and they didn't jump out of the way as I lumbered through. They just sat and stared. And there were toads, too, brown and knobby, hopping slowly across the path.

At some point it became clear that reaching Middleburgh by evening was not feasible. By late afternoon I had covered only twenty miles from Route 23. While the Catskills were now in the rearview mirror, it didn't feel like my pace was getting any faster. Rather, it felt like I was slowing down. The hills were steep, the trail was overgrown, and my energy was sagging.

At this pace, finishing the course in seven days was not going to happen. And that meant problems, because my food supply was fixed, indeed barely adequate for seven days, let alone eight, or nine, or more. Without more calories, my pace would slow to a crawl, if I could keep moving at all.

I had meant to complete the through-run on a "self-supported" basis, meaning that I would rely on my caches and whatever food I could buy along the way, without receiving support from other people. If you receive help from others, then your through-run is considered "supported." There's nothing wrong with that, it's just a different category that is considered not quite as difficult. Now I made a quick mental calculation: self-supported was not going to work. As much as I had wanted this journey to be an exercise in individual initiative, it was time to call in the cavalry. It was time to ask for help.

I pulled out my phone, and luck was with me—there was enough cell signal for me to get through to Sue. She didn't sound surprised at my slowing pace, and when I asked for help, she agreed to meet me with a resupply. We identified a link-up point about ten miles down the trail where it crossed a paved road. She could reach this in a few hours. This resupply would clearly violate the rules for a self-supported through-run. But I could, if I finished the course, still claim the record on a supported basis. And that seemed better than crawling through the forest on hands and knees.

With this plan in place, I felt much relieved, and soldiered on through the dark, dank forest with fresh resolve. Toward dusk, the path reached a steep gravel road that led down below to the intersection where I'd meet Sue. Downhill meant picking up the pace, albeit gingerly, as my wet feet were sensitive to the rocks and gravel. Also, I was careful not to step on the thousands of red efts that covered the road. Small salamanders about one to two inches long and bright orange with red dots, these creatures move very slowly. A couple of them looked up at me as if to challenge my presence in their territory. The rest ignored me.

Reaching the paved road at the foot of the hill, I looked around for our car but didn't see it. Not wanting to lose time, I spotted the next blaze, turned left on the road, and kept moving. After a minute or two, Sue appeared and pulled over into a dirt lane to park. And not a moment too soon, as a flash of lightning was followed immediately by thunder and heavy rain. I ducked into the car and was happy to see not only Sue but also Philip. They had brought a large pizza and a bottle of beer. I shoved slice after slice into my mouth and guzzled the beer, shifting uncomfortably in my damp clothes in the cramped back seat.

We talked about the Catskills, which I had just passed through, the town of Middleburgh, where I was headed, and the Schoharie Valley, the wild and strange place where we currently found ourselves, while the rained drummed on the car's roof and splashed all around. Philip handed me another slice. Didn't he want it? He waved his hand. What impression this crazy adventure made on him, it was hard to tell.

By the time I had eaten my fill, it was dark outside. It was great to see Sue and Philip, and it would have been nice to stay longer. But if I didn't keep moving, the accumulated fatigue was going to catch up with me and knock me into a stupor. And there was still a long ways to go. And the clock was still ticking.

All too soon, I hopped back out of the car and headed out into the rain. Sue had brought me a new garbage bag, and I stretched it over my body. Still digesting the meal, I walked for a bit, flashlight playing across the trees and telephone poles on the side of the road, constantly searching for the next blaze, and always worried that I would miss a turn.

A few houses sat alongside the road, many dark and quiet, but in some there were lights and voices. In one dwelling, images were splashed across an inner wall, clearly from a television set or computer monitor. In other places, music and voices wafted out in the night air, as if a party were in progress. I peered into windows, wondering what kind of people lived inside, whether they were having a good time, whether they'd be friendly toward a stranger stopping by for a quick visit. Just a traveler looking for a chance to dry off and escape the solitude of the nighttime road.

I needed to keep moving. I power-walked on the uphills and broke into a very slow jog on the downhills, ever mindful of my sensitive feet.

West Conesville wasn't much more than an intersection, and it was pitch dark and dead quiet when I arrived. Hanging a left, I crossed a bridge and arrived at a point where the trail turned onto private property. According to the notes, this section of the Long Path followed a logging road, but in the darkness the road, if that's what it was, was indistinguishable from the soft and muddy ground. Rocks and branches were mixed into the dirt, as if the area had been chewed up by large machines. The road lay on a slope that stretched down to a stream, and the footing was slanted, not level. This began to play havoc with my left ankle and strained calf muscle. I limped forward one step at a time, in what was now a steady downpour, searching for the next blaze.

The blazes were becoming increasingly difficult to follow. Some of them seemed a little off. If I stood with my back to the tree with the most recent blaze and looked straight forward, there was nothing in view. After a brief search, the next blaze turned out to be somewhat to the left and uphill, and the next one after that was somewhat to the right and downhill, as if the trail crew had been dizzy or disoriented when they marked this section.

I pulled out the notes, sheltering them under a plastic bag to keep them from getting soaked in the rain. The notes referenced stone walls, survey markers, maple syrup tubes—but these were not visible in the darkness, or when I did catch a glimpse of something, it was impossible to relate it to the notes or figure out the location. My pace slowed to a crawl.

After the Catskills I had hoped to catch a break, I thought to myself bitterly, but here things were, if anything, getting worse. At this rate, I'd never finish.

I stumbled forward with growing anxiety. At the next blaze, nothing was visible to the front but an impenetrable thicket of saplings and brambles. I dialed up the highest power setting on the flashlight, mindful that this would quickly drain the batteries, and played the beam in a 180-degree arc. But there were no blazes. Exploring to the right and downhill, there was nothing. I turned around and headed back uphill. Nothing. I marched out to the tangle of brush and poked around its edges. It was impassable. I went back to the last blaze, and repeated the entire sequence. Nothing.

There was nothing more to do. My enthusiasm and energy suddenly collapsed, like a building that tumbles to the ground in a great cloud of dust once explosive charges have demolished its support. This was the end of the line. The Long Path had finally gotten the best of me. It did have a mischievous personality, as my friend Todd had warned. No, it was downright malicious. The people who designed this trail didn't want you to finish it, or they didn't care. Or perhaps they did care, but some malevolent spirit counteracted their efforts—the same spirit that had knocked down so many trees on the southern outskirts of the Catskills. Maybe it was the Devil, I muttered to myself, seeking to rationalize this pathetic situation. Maybe the entire Long Path is his private domain.

The rain beat down steadily as I considered my options. I had made it more than 250 miles out of the 350-mile distance, and my friends would view this as a major accomplishment. They wouldn't care if I didn't complete the entire trail.

Well, with that decided, maybe I could finally relax.

Then I imagined David O'Neill, the current Long Path record holder, congratulating me on the effort. A friendly and gracious man, he wouldn't needle me or remind me of his warning to beware the northern sections. He'd be a gentleman about it. And the record would still be his. This thought left a bitter taste in my mouth. I had to think of something.

In desperation, I pulled out the cellphone, thinking I might be able to figure out my location using the map function and perhaps follow a compass heading. Remarkably, there was enough signal here for the map function to identify my location and display the nearby roads. But the display didn't show the Long Path, and the roads it identified weren't mentioned in the notes. I couldn't figure out which way to go.

I stood in the rain, wet, unhappy, confused, and pondering what to do, when I noticed a text message. It was from Todd, wishing me good luck on this next section of the trail. The message was time stamped around 10:00 p.m. According to my watch, it was now a little after 11:00. I took a chance and dialed his phone number. Todd answered on the first ring. Explaining the situation, I asked if he could see my current location from the SPOT signal and figure out which way to go. After a moment or two, Todd came back on the line. He told me to keep going in the same direction and I would reach a road. Enormously grateful to Todd, I headed out, skirted the thicket, and immediately saw the next blaze behind it.

Winston Churchill once said, "When you're going through hell, don't stop." Thanks to Todd, I was able to keep going.

In due course the path emerged from the awful wooded slope onto welcome pavement. I started to run down the road, but now my feet really hurt, and I slowed to a walk. I glanced to the left and made out a large body of water. This was the Schoharie Reservoir, the northernmost reservoir in the New York City water supply. From here up to six hundred million gallons of water per day flow south through the eighteen-mile Shandaken tunnel, which penetrates the bedrock of the Catskill mountains and empties into the Esopus Creek near the town of Phoenicia, which I had passed through two long days ago. From there, the water runs seven miles to the Ashokan Reservoir (visible from the top of Slide Mountain) and thence through the Catskill Aqueduct to New York City. When it was constructed in the 1920s, the Shandaken tunnel was the longest in the world. Today it no longer ranks in the top one hundred. However, the New York City water supply system continues to claim the world's longest tunnel, the Delaware Aqueduct, which stretches 83.8 miles from the western Catskills to a reservoir just north of the city.

The surface of the Schoharie Reservoir was still and black. There were buildings and vehicles in one area, and on the far side a series of boulders laid out in rows. The notes explained that these were pieces of petrified wood that had been excavated during the construction of the reservoir in the 1920s. Apparently, these chunks of wood included fossils of the Gilboa tree (*Eospermatopteris*), the oldest-known prehistoric tree. Growing to a height of twenty-five feet, the Gilboa tree superficially resembles a fern or palm tree. It grew some 385 million years ago, long before mammals and dinosaurs, during the period when the first "greening" of the planet's surface was taking place. This spot in the Schoharie Valley was apparently one of the earth's first forests.

According to Robert Titus, a geologist who's studied the Catskills, if you could hop in a time machine to visit the ancient forest of Gilboa trees on a windless day, it would be a strange experience. It would have been eerily quiet. You would not have heard the song of the hermit thrush, because birds had not yet evolved. The insects were so primitive they had no ability to make noise.

The road reached the bottom of the dam, turned left, crossed a bridge over the outlet, and headed uphill. I didn't realize it at the time, but only a short distance away lay the town of Roxbury, where John Burroughs had spent his childhood. His grave was located at his childhood home, about ten miles to the southwest. Next to the grave is a glacial erratic, a large sandstone boulder that Burroughs called "Boyhood Rock." As a child he had played by the rock, and as an old man, he used to sit on it, entertaining guests with stories or simply admiring the forest. The surface of Boyhood Rock is covered with small holes, the fossil casts of roots belonging to ancient Gilboa trees, which had grown in river sediment that had hardened over time into sandstone.

⌒

After the scare by the thicket, I was once again carefully following each step in the notes, hoping to avoid further confusion. With some concern, I read that the Long Path had been rerouted due to storm damage from Hurricane Irene. Notes clutched in one hand, flashlight in the other, I followed the blazes onto Stryker Road, which parallels the Schoharie Creek. The notes identified a large farm to the left. I squinted in the darkness and saw the outlines of a barn. Then the notes described a large overhanging rock that extends over Schoharie Creek. I peered into the darkness but could see nothing. There was a deep gully through which the stream presumably flowed. But the depths were invisible.

According to the notes, the next objective was Nickerson's Campground, which lay 0.8 miles along Stryker Road. This seemed easy enough, and I walked along feeling confident—until a barrier marked

"Road Closed" barred the way. This was a bit of a surprise. There was nothing in the notes about barriers or closed roads. It seemed odd to omit such an important feature. Nonetheless, I walked around the barrier and continued along the pavement, a grassy slope to my left, while on my right the Schoharie Creek coursed through the deep ravine, hidden in inky darkness. And now there was another barrier. Again the notes came out, but there was still no mention of a closed road. Feeling less confident, I climbed over the second barrier.

Suppose the road had been closed recently, and the notes had not yet been updated to reflect this change. Then what?

Then I'd be screwed.

Suddenly my foot slipped on dirt and loose rocks. I flashed the light around and saw that the road was washed out. The surface sloped downward and to the right, where there was a very dark spot—undoubtedly a sheer drop into the ravine. I inched my way through the washout, avoiding the right side of the road with great care. After a few more steps, the pavement resumed. There was a barrier and then a second one, a mirror image of what I had just passed. The road kept dragging on. Surely the distance had been covered already. But there was no sign of the campground. I felt disoriented and apprehensive.

Then an intersection appeared out of the mist. This couldn't be right. I sat down on the ground in despair. Nothing in the notes indicated an intersection. I should have reached the campground long ago.

In desperation, I pulled out the cellphone. There wasn't enough signal for the mapping function to access the Internet. I saw the text message that Todd had sent me earlier and thought of calling him again. But it was now 2:00 a.m. It wouldn't have been right to disturb him. He had already gone out of his way to help me. I couldn't take advantage of him every time I was confused—that wasn't the right way to treat a friend. This was my adventure, after all, and I was going to have to figure it out on my own.

I picked up the phone again, intending to shut it down, as the battery life was a precious resource. A breeze tickled my cheek, and perhaps the atmospheric conditions changed at that moment just enough for a signal to slip through. I saw that the mapping function had populated the screen with my location and the surrounding roads. Nickerson's Campground was two hundred yards away.

A streetlight illuminated the entrance to the campground and a large building, which was evidently a general store. I sat down on a retaining wall and ate a quick snack. The aqua blazes were painted on the side of the building and pointed to a dirt road that looped behind the campground. Back on track again, my spirits were significantly improved, and I walked briskly down the road, notes clutched in one hand, determined to stay on top of my location and ready for the next turn. The road reentered the campground, and the course notes became complicated.

"Bear right," the notes said, then "bear right" again, then "turn left at campsite 572," and after a bit "turn right at campsite 546." I flashed my light around and saw large trailers parked in the grass, but I couldn't make out numbers. I was going to have to walk directly up to each campsite and hunt for the numbers. The people sleeping inside might not like that.

Someone was walking down the path toward me. A man approached, and I saw a patch on his shoulder labeled "security." Great, I thought to myself, now I'm going to be arrested.

But this individual didn't pull out handcuffs. Instead, he introduced himself as Doug, the owner of the campground. And, sure, he knew all about the Long Path. He pointed the way. I was enormously relieved.

Doug had one favor to ask. As I followed the blazes back towards the Schoharie Creek, there was an area with people sleeping in tents. Would I mind taking a shortcut around them, so as not to disturb their slumber? Of course, I replied graciously, nodding my head and smiling. I asked him to repeat the directions, but I couldn't understand a word he said. My head felt like it was spinning and bouncing, as if I had become a human bobble-head. Maybe it was the lack of sleep—although to be honest, it's a struggle to remember directions on the best of days. Doug repeated the directions, and I just kept nodding and smiling (and bobbling).

Thanking Doug, I strode out after the aqua blazes and arrived a few minutes later at an area with many tents. I marched straight through, feeling bad to have let Doug down. But there was no way I was going to take even one step off the path.

The trail soon passed by waterfalls in the Minekill State Park, and the sound of rushing water rose from the depths, but nothing was visible except a cliff edge to my right, which I carefully avoided. At one point, the path crossed a stream and headed up a muddy embankment. I charged up the slope, slipped, and fell back. Caught on a branch, my precious flashlight was ripped from its nylon cord and thrown into the brush.

I was immediately sunk in despair. Without that light source, I'd never be able to finish the course. This was one disaster too many. It was time to call it quits, this time for good. I sat in the mud, head in hands. After a bit, I forced myself to take a deep breath. Then I clicked on my headlamp. In a minute or two, I found the flashlight, tied it back on to its cord, and crawled up the embankment. Panic had been averted, a shaky calm reestablished.

Moving through the darkness, I lost track of time. Sometime later, the sky began to lighten. I was running through a field, the grass soaking wet. The trees were surrounded by frames and wire mesh to keep out deer. According to the notes, this was the Lansing Manor Visitor Center. Apparently, there was a building that had been built in 1819 by John Lansing, Jr., one of New York's representatives to the Constitutional Convention of 1787. Today it is operated by the New York Power Authority, the same agency that pushed through the Marcy South power lines, whose concrete and steel towers I had admired so many days and miles ago. Why a power agency would operate a historical site wasn't clear, but there wasn't anyone around to ask.

The path took me to a covered picnic area, which seemed perfect for a break. Off came the shoes and socks. This time it wasn't just a case of wrinkled skin. Now there were blisters, located between the toes and the balls of each foot, the likes of which I couldn't recall in more than twenty years of hiking and running. Out came the blister kit. Fumbling with wipes, bandages, tape, and a small scissors, I drained the blisters and bandaged them as best I could. Then it was time to rehydrate a camping meal.

The night had been one disaster after another: the impassable thicket, the washed-out road, confusion at the campground, losing my flashlight, constant rain and wet ground, and now blisters. Since linking up with Sue and Philip, I had covered barely twenty miles, at a pace no better than a slow crawl. Not only had I not gotten the hoped-for break after the Catskills, things had gotten demonstrably worse.

On a positive note, Middleburgh was less than twenty-five miles away, and with some luck I might make it there by late afternoon, in time for pizza at Hubie's. Their pizza was really good. That was something to aim for. Thinking about anything else seemed pointless.

I stretched out on a park bench, giving my feet a few minutes to dry off. I closed my eyes, hoping to catch a few minutes of rest. A mosquito whined about me. The repellant seemed to keep it away, but the insect was persistent: it kept circling, probing for weakness.

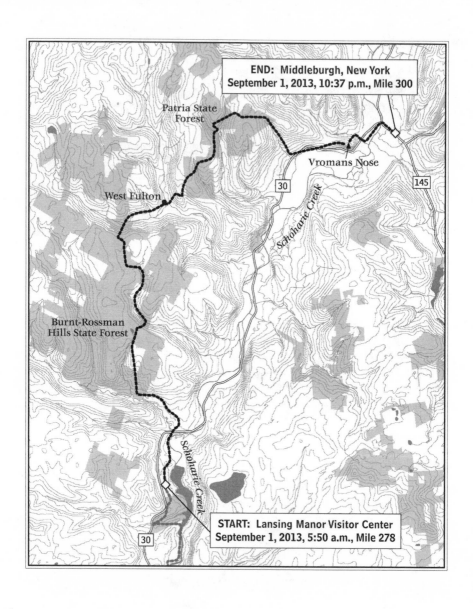

END: Middleburgh, New York
September 1, 2013, 10:37 p.m., Mile 300

Patria State
Forest

Vromans Nose

30

145

West Fulton

Schoharie Creek

Burnt-Rossman
Hills State Forest

Schoharie Creek

START: Lansing Manor Visitor Center
September 1, 2013, 5:50 a.m., Mile 278

30

Chapter 10

Limping into Middleburgh

However sweet these laid-up stores, however convenient this
   dwelling we cannot remain here,
However shelter'd this port and however calm these waters we
   must not anchor here,
However welcome the hospitality that surrounds us we are not
   permitted to receive it but a little while.

—Walt Whitman, "Song of the Open Road"

The book of nature is like a page written over or printed upon with
different-sized characters and in many different languages, interlined
and cross-lined, and with a great variety of marginal notes and refer-
ences. . . . It is a book which he reads best who goes most slowly or
even tarries long by the way.

—John Burroughs, "The Art of Seeing Things"

Lansing Manor Visitor Center, Sunday, September 1, 2013, 5:50 a.m.

Despite the repellant, the mosquito kept circling around my head and
whining in my ear. I sighed and sat up.

A car drove through the parking lot. It would have been nice for
someone to get out and walk over to the picnic area to say hello. But
no one did.

Just keep moving, I told myself, that's all you have to do.

After exiting the visitor center, the trail took me uphill along a rocky path through a forest of deciduous hardwoods. The notes acknowledged that there were no views here, but pointed out interesting sights, including abandoned sawmills and unnamed ponds. These didn't seem interesting to me—it was an undistinguished trail by a stream through the woods. Without any particular features, there was nothing to look at, no goals to aim for. Without landmarks, I couldn't judge progress. To pass the time, I tried counting steps, but lost track. I power-walked as best I could, but my left ankle and calf were feeling the strain. I became irritated and anxious.

After a long time, the trail passed a cemetery. I had long ago lost count of the number of cemeteries situated on the Long Path, and barely gave this one a glance. On a positive note, if I dropped dead, they wouldn't have to carry my body far.

The notes mentioned the path would pass by the childhood home of Henry Conklin, who had grown up in this area in the 1830s and written a memoir about his early life—a sort of northern Catskills equivalent of *Little House on the Prairie*. Focused on the ground in front of my feet, I didn't notice the cabin by the side of the trail. But afterward, I read his memoirs and learned that in 1832, when Conklin was born, the Schoharie Valley was just as sparsely settled and just as much a frontier as the Ohio Valley. In the book, Conklin tells of his mother cooking dinner over an open fireplace: "Stoves had not been invented then or if they had the people were too poor to buy them." Young Conklin didn't have shoes until he was twelve, but that didn't stop him from running around barefoot in search of flowers, leeks, and berries. In the snow his feet would turn as red as goose feet. "Oh horrors," he recalled, "how they would ache and smart while holding them up to the fireplace."

His father moved the family frequently, constantly in search of a better farm and more opportunity, but he didn't always make the best judgments, especially when he drank. As a child, Conklin was conscious of his family's poverty. "We might have went to the poor house," he wrote, "but there was none to go to." In his words, the Schoharie Valley was a wilderness of "want" and "work." But he and his family were happy. The book opens with some simple advice: "You may get down and pray all your life for something but if you don't put forth any effort or work with your prayer and faith you will never accomplish anything."

〜

Eventually the trail emerged from the forest and arrived in West Fulton, an intersection in a valley between steep hills with a handful of houses, but no restaurants, gas stations, or delis—in other words, no food. There was a little park by a church, and I spread out in the grass by a picnic area. Wet shoes came off, and I wrung a few ounces of water out of the socks, then stretched them out to dry in the weak sunlight. Then I bent over my feet, dried them off, and redressed the blisters. A fellow came out of the church and we chatted for a minute. I dozed off in midsentence.

Sometime later I opened my eyes and saw that the sky had turned hazy. A few raindrops spattered against the ground. I swept up the small pile of bandages and wrappers and gathered together my belongings. It was now early afternoon, and with something like twenty miles to go, I'd need to hurry if I wanted to get pizza at Hubie's.

The trail headed back up into the hills. I groaned out loud. Why did the Long Path always head back up into the hills? Why not just follow the stream at the bottom of the valley—even better, stick to the road for a few miles! But that was not to be. Instead, the aqua blazes led me along an endless slope through a featureless forest of maple and beech. My left ankle was now quite stiff. I compensated by turning the foot outward, which took some of the strain off the joint, but slowed my pace even further.

My energy was sagging. I downed an entire chocolate bar, which, according to the label, contained at least a thousand calories. But it didn't do anything for me. Middleburgh was getting no closer.

I started to worry. How would I make it from Middleburgh to the finish, another fifty long miles, with only one day's worth of food?

The idea of running the Long Path in seven days had become a thing of the past, just like the goal of completing it on a self-supported basis. All of a sudden, eight days seemed like a stretch. With growing dismay, I realized that the closer I got to the end, the more I was slowing down, and thus the longer it might take to finish. In theory, I could make it to the finish in eleven days and still beat the prior record of twelve days, even if I had to crawl on hands and knees. But I didn't have that much time. Today was Sunday. I was supposed to fly to Tennessee Tuesday night for business meetings on Wednesday. That flight could be pushed to Wednesday morning, but no later. Otherwise, my personal achievement would come at the expense of commitments I had made to teammates. That wasn't the right way to do things.

Suddenly there was a flash of light directly overhead, followed almost instantaneously by a crack of thunder. The rain poured hard, drenching my clothes. I stopped, got a long-sleeve shirt from my pack, and pulled it on over my head. It kept off some of the chill. But the rain ran down my arms and back and through my shorts, soaking me thoroughly.

I took one step forward, breathed heavily, then took another step, like a mountaineer climbing an icy slope at high altitude. Indeed I had experienced this pace before—my thoughts jumped back to a mountaineering trip in South America many years ago. At the end of three weeks of trekking through Bolivia's altiplano, there was to be a final climb up Mount Illimani, a peak 21,266 feet high. I was the only client who stayed for this part of the trip. The guides sat me down for a talk. Since I was the only client, they explained, there was no need to push myself to keep up with others. Indeed, they cautioned, people were sometimes so intent on reaching the summit, and pushed themselves so hard to get there, that they became exhausted. This left them in bad shape for the descent, and that's when the accidents happened. Gesturing to a crevasse at eighteen thousand feet, one of the guides explained that a few years ago, an inexperienced climber had slipped on the way down from Illimani's summit and dragged the rest of his group into that crevasse. Half died from the impact, he mentioned casually, and the other half froze to death. What he needed me to do was exercise some judgment.

"Judgment." I said the word out loud, rolling it around on my tongue as if I were practicing a foreign language. "Judgment," I repeated. What does judgment mean? It means quitting is sometimes the smarter option.

An idea formed in my mind, an honorable way out of this nightmare. Because of work commitments, I would explain to friends, and because of my slowing pace (I was injured, after all), quitting here was the right thing to do. I wasn't some juvenile adventurer. As a mature fifty-year-old, I had responsibilities. I understood where my duties lay, and it was the correct *judgment* not to continue.

Now that this was decided, I felt giddy with relief and started to imagine sleeping in a bed, feeling warm and dry, drinking beer, eating a slice of pizza (and not just any pizza, but a slice with pepperoni and mushrooms from Hubie's). Friends would be impressed with my three-hundred-mile jaunt through the woods—they wouldn't care whether I finished the entire Long Path or just most of it. What difference would it make? After all, I had raised money for a good cause. That was more important than a record—a record that appealed only to my personal vanity, and one that would be broken as soon as a serious athlete took an interest in the Long Path.

The tension accumulated over seven days of intense effort began slowly to drain away.

Then my thoughts drifted back, once again, to the current record holder, David O'Neill. He was a good guy, he would be gracious—why, he had warned me about the northern sections of the Long Path. He would totally understand.

The imaginary pizza I had been savoring turned to dust in my mouth.

Dammit, I didn't care about being dry or sleeping in a bed or eating pizza. None of that mattered. My quest might be ridiculous (that much seemed indisputable), but it was something I had started, and therefore it was something I ought to finish. If it were that easy, then everyone would hold records.

The rain lifted as I slowly neared the summit. I pulled the cellphone from the plastic bag in which it was wrapped, hoping that with some altitude, I might catch enough signal to get a call through. To my surprise, I reached Sue on the first try.

"I'm moving slowly," I explained, voicing out loud the concerns that had been weighing on my mind. "I'm concerned about finishing. I don't think I'm getting enough calories. I'm worried that I won't have enough food to get to the end."

Sue wasn't surprised. The evening before, when she and Philip had brought me pizza, she had remarked on how much weight I had lost. I was starting to look "skeletal," she said. If I could make it to Middleburgh, she would meet me there the next morning and spend the day with me, providing food and supplies at various points along the route.

I breathed a sigh of relief. Once again, my wife was coming to the rescue—bringing not only needed sustenance, but a few hours of companionship on what had become an increasingly lonely journey. If I succeeded in finishing the trail and setting the record, much of the credit would be due to her support.

Now it was time to check the voicemail on my phone. I had noticed the indicator a few days ago, but hadn't retrieved the message, not wanting to be distracted by issues from the outside world. Punching the PIN, I suddenly heard the voice of my boss, the CEO of our company. Evidently he had discovered what I was up to.

"I understand you're taking on quite a challenge," I heard him say. "I'm calling to wish you good luck."

That message boosted my morale immensely. Having workmates and family behind me made all the difference in the world.

In much better spirits, I made it down the mountain and arrived on a paved road. It was now late afternoon. Through the mists and low-lying clouds, the Schoharie Valley was spread out in front of me, looking like a postcard scene from the Alps.

I hurried along the paved road, trotting briskly, focusing on form, trying to ignore my blistered feet, which were burning with each step, and mindful that I had business in Middleburgh. It was getting dark, and I wasn't sure when Hubie's would close.

Yes, pizza had become a fixation. I don't eat pizza very often any more, preferring healthier fare, but like a lot of Americans, I grew up on the stuff. At one of my first hundred-mile races, I had made it to the fifty-mile point, only to collapse in a chair, feeling weak and nauseous. My nutrition plan was based on a specially formulated energy drink that was supposed to contain a balanced mix of nutrients. I would mix the powder with water, shake it vigorously to get rid of the lumps, and then throw in a chocolate gel to give it some taste. There are elite athletes who can pound this stuff for hours on end. But at that point in the race, I couldn't stomach another sip. "This is one tough race," I declared in a squeaky voice.

My coach, and the race director, Lisa Smith-Batchen, cut me short: "There are many tougher races." She would know. She is an elite marathon and ultramarathon runner, an Ironman, and a nine-time Badwater finisher who had won the race twice. She would go on to become the first woman to run the Badwater Quad, a 584-mile odyssey through Death Valley.

Then her tone lightened, "Hey Ken, have a slice of pizza." I did, and it revived me.

Back in July, I had ventured out to the Schoharie Valley to scout a section of the Long Path. Afterward, having discovered Hubie's and gotten halfway through a pepperoni pizza, I noticed at the next table a gentleman wearing a Trail Conference hat. That gentleman turned out to be Drew Adams. A former noncommissioned officer in the 10th Mountain Division, he and I were soon swapping stories about our army days (we both know what it's like to sleep on the ground wrapped in a poncho liner). He had generously offered to let me not only stash my final drop bag on his porch, but spend the night in his house.

Now that I was hurrying along the last few miles to Middleburgh, there was only one wrinkle in this plan: I couldn't find Drew's phone number. Out came the cellphone. I punched in directory assistance and carefully spelled his name and his address, but according to the operator, there was no listing.

How could that be? I tried to explain to the operator that I had not only met Drew at Hubie's, but I had stopped by his house to drop off my bag just a few days ago. He had to be a real person. So I called Hubie's and asked if they knew Drew. No luck. The situation had become surreal.

Perplexed, I put away the cellphone and hurried along. In any case, before I got to Middleburgh, there was one last obstacle: a six-hundred-foot rocky protuberance in the middle of Schoharie Valley called Vrooman's Nose. Named "Onistagrawa" or "Corn Mountain" by the Mohawk Indians, this small mountain got its moniker from Adam Vrooman—and not because of the size of his nose (as I had first imagined), but simply because in 1711 he had purchased six hundred acres from the Mohawks, including the nose-shaped mountain. The deed was executed by chiefs representing the Bear, Wolf, and Turtle clans (the document bears small hand-drawn representations of their respective mascots) and then properly ratified by the British governor, and all was well for a period of time.

However, some sixty-nine years later, during the Revolutionary War, the Mohawks returned to the Schoharie Valley, but now as allies of the British. In 1780, the Mohawk war chief Joseph Brant (Thayendanegea) led a raid into the Schoharie Valley, whose fertile land and productive farms had become an important source of provisions for the Revolutionary army.

Joseph Brant was a shrewd battlefield leader with a colorful past. As a young boy, he had participated in a battle in what became known as the French and Indian Wars and later admitted he was so scared by the clatter of musketry that he clutched onto a slender sapling near his position and held on for dear life. But with experience, his confidence and audacity grew, and later it was said of him that he had "fought with Death and dulled his sword."

As a young man, he was described as modest, serious, and exceedingly kind, with a judicious mind and fearless heart. Over time, he was recognized as a chieftain of the Mohawks by virtue of merit rather than birth. Brant was called a "Pine-tree Chief," that is, one who soars strong and tall above his peers.

Brant proved himself to be one of the most successful leaders in the guerilla warfare that the British and their Native American allies waged on American forces in outlying areas. Some said he possessed a "remarkable genius in the art of stratagem." Others accused him of wanton cruelty. The settlers looked on Brant as a ruthless marauder, thirsting for blood. He acknowledged, according to a source, that during one raid, he was unable to restrain the ferocity of his warriors, who "sped into the doomed village like hounds let slip from their leashes."

In the summer of 1780, a mixed force of British regulars, Rangers, and native warriors under Brant appeared in the Schoharie Valley. A few settlers were caught by surprise and killed, including some women and children. About thirty persons were taken captive. The marauders moved up the valley, burning farms, running off the livestock, and destroying an estimated hundred thousand bushels of wheat, but they were unable to capture small forts near Middleburgh and Vrooman's Nose.

After the Revolutionary War ended, Brant journeyed to England to plead for assistance for the Mohawks and their Iroquois brethren, who had remained staunch allies of the British through thick and thin. A British courtier admired Brant's "half military and half savage costume" and described him as "manly and intelligent" with a disposition that was very mild. "His manners are polished: he expressed himself with fluency, and was much esteemed." Brought into the presence of King George III, Brant stated "I bow to no man as I am considered a prince among my people, but I will gladly shake your hand."

As compensation for their losses, the British provided the Mohawks with land in Ontario, Canada. Brant and his followers settled on the banks of the Great River. Today this area is part of the Six Nations Reservation, and nearby can be found the town of Brantford. Brant lived out his years in a two-story house, and as an old man took great pleasure in watching the Mohawk youth participate in sports. On his deathbed, he said, "Have pity on the poor Indians. If you can get any influence with the great, endeavor to do them all the good you can."

Today Vrooman's Nose is called the "Sky Island of the Schoharie Valley." In 1983, some of the valley's local inhabitants, including descendants of the original Vroomans, raised funds to preserve the Nose for posterity.

Not surprisingly, the path followed a very steep grade as it mounted what might be considered one of the nostrils of this six-hundred-foot tall nose. It was exactly the kind of gratuitous side trip up and over a steep hill that the Long Path couldn't resist.

This had to be the work of Long Path cochairmen and trail builders extraordinaire, Andy Garrison and Jakob Franke. I imagined myself challenging them: "Haven't you guys heard of the shortest distance between two points?"

They would have responded: "How could you walk past Vrooman's Nose and not want to go up and see the view?"

The narrow trail up Vrooman's Nose had a grade of thirty degrees or perhaps even more. Needless to say, my ankle didn't appreciate being asked to flex to this degree, and my calf began to ache under the strain. So I dug in with the poles, determined to hoist myself to the top through upper body strength alone, if that's what it would take. Then I felt a sharp pain in my shoulder. I went back to focusing on each step, one at a time, with my left foot turned outward to ease some of the strain.

The top of Vrooman's Nose is called the "dance floor." It is composed of a hard sandstone cap that was polished during the last ice age by a southward-moving glacier. During daylight there are reportedly beautiful views across the Schoharie Valley, but in the darkness the landscape appeared vast and empty, marked only by an occasional light sparkling in the distance. I limped across the dance floor, conscious of large spaces all around me and mindful that there must be a cliff edge, and beyond it a steep drop.

Legend has it that Revolutionary War hero Tim Murphy was carrying two pails of buttermilk across the top of Vrooman's Nose when he was surprised by Mohawk braves. He leaped over the edge, landed far down the slope, and ran all the way back to his farm, where he had left his rifle, without spilling a drop of milk. I on the other hand stumbled down the path at a very slow pace.

Eventually the trail deposited me on the paved road on the valley floor. Middleburgh was just ahead: I could almost see the town, and I could just about taste the pizza.

But there was still three or four miles to go, and this next section had a questionable reputation. While planning the run, I had noticed comments posted on the Trail Conference website indicating that the path into Middleburgh was a little rough. One comment in particular had caught my attention:

[T]he trail becomes nearly non-existent. . . . The corn crop is towering at 8–9 ft high and the undergrowth is over my head between the corn and hedgerow to my right. . . . Paint blazes are hard to find. If it weren't for someone riding a 4 wheeler down thru the trail lately I probably couldn't have found any trail at all. Every once in a while when not sure of where I was, I would beat back the brush to the hedgerow and find the Aqua Blaze on a tree. . . . This part is also heavily overgrown and trekking poles help push back the undergrowth and keep your balance on the uneven terrain.

I had read this with raised eyebrows. The fellow's evident frustration made him sound like an inexperienced hiker, a "newbie" who wasn't comfortable on a surface that wasn't neatly groomed. Whatever might lurk ahead, I wasn't afraid of a cornfield—not when food and rest lay only a few miles away.

Sure enough, the trail soon veered off the road and headed along a hedgerow beside a cornfield. The path quickly narrowed into an alleyway, hemmed in by thick vegetation on both sides. The ground was muddy, and my feet were once again wet. The cornstalks were quite tall, and I began to feel claustrophobic. And even though there was nowhere to go but forward, I grew anxious after each blaze until the next one came into view.

I pursed my lips and began to "power-breath"—a technique I had learned on that South American mountaineering trip so many years ago. The purpose of power-breathing is to force more oxygen into the lungs, a helpful technique when at high altitude. Right now I wasn't short of air. Rather, I concentrated on my breathing to keep my frustration from boiling over.

So close to Middleburgh! What the hell was the Long Path doing here mucking about in a muddy alleyway between a cornfield and a creek? Who in their right mind would come out to hike on a path like this? Who in their right mind would design a path like this?

I scanned ahead for the next blaze. To be fair, there wasn't really a place to put one. You can't very well paint a blaze on a cornstalk. After a bit, I spotted a tiny splash of aqua paint on the thin branch of a bush. This was pathetic. I found myself getting really angry.

A broken stalk leaned across the path, barring my way. I took this as a personal affront and raised a trekking pole to strike it down. But an image appeared in my mind of the pole shattering into thousands of lightweight carbon fragments. There were millions of cornstalks, too many to battle. I lowered the pole and trudged on, weary and dispirited. The power-breathing wasn't calming me down. I began to groan in frustration, and then I started cursing out loud.

"I get it," I shouted as I slogged through the mud, dodging cornstalks. "No one would ever want to hike here. The Long Path is just a big joke. To see if anyone would be stupid enough to come out here and give it a try. And the joke is on me!"

It's a good thing no one was hanging around in the cornfield, listening to me rant and rave. They would have thought I was a lunatic.

I'm especially glad that Long Path cochairmen Andy and Jakob weren't there. Andy would have stared at me through his spectacles with an impish grin on his face, his expression conveying the strong opinion that people who bite off more than they can chew have no one to blame but themselves. Jakob would have explained patiently, as if talking to a child, that anything is better than a road walk. It would have been embarrassing.

The cornfield went on much longer than it should have. Eventually the path emerged into an open area, and I could see the road into town. Abandoning the blazes, I bolted for the road, running through a field (wet grass soaking shoes of course) and then onto pavement, and now finally I was striding across the bridge into Middleburgh. The bridge was festooned in lights, but the historic structures and old-fashioned store fronts lining Main Street were dark. It was 10:30 p.m., and alas, Hubie's had long since closed.

I had missed out on pizza, but there was a gas-station convenience store with a large choice of unhealthy but high-calorie items on the shelves. Determined not to repeat past mistakes, I reached for a jar of applesauce, a Danish, a box of Pop-Tarts, some kind of plastic-wrapped hot dog, and a can of Spaghetti-Os. The cashier was impressed by my story. He tossed in a candy bar for free.

At least I had food. The only remaining question was whether Drew and his wife Cheryl would be at home—assuming they weren't figments of my imagination. If they were away, I could still sleep on their porch—assuming the house wasn't also a figment of my imagination. Just in case, as I walked past each house along the street, I sized up its porch and looked for signs of occupation. Would the inhabitants mind a stranger sheltering for a few hours out of the rain? Or would they call the police? I pictured the cruiser pulling up to the curb, a burly officer emerging, in one hand a TASER, in the other the leash to a snarling German Shepherd.

As it turned out, Drew's house was standing exactly where it was supposed to be. I pushed the doorbell. No answer. My watch read nearly 11:00 p.m. a little late for an unannounced social call. A minute went by. I pushed the doorbell again. There was a loud party going on down the street. Maybe I could hang out with drunk teenagers while I dined on my Pop-Tarts and Sphagetti-Os.

Then the door swung open, and there to my great relief was Cheryl. Not only did she welcome me in, she heated up some leftover chicken and rice and offered me a bowl of homemade applesauce. It was the best I had ever tasted. I had three bowls. At the same time, Pop Tarts started disappearing into my stomach, followed by the plastic-wrapped hot dog, the can of Spaghetti-Os, and the jar of store-bought applesauce (not nearly as good as hers). I took a hot shower for the first time in a week. My clothes went into the wash and shoes got propped up against a fan to dry out. Cheryl showed me to a room with a real bed, also the first I'd seen in a week.

Before sleep, however, I needed to plan. Out came the course notes. Fifty miles to go. Fifty miles! That seemed manageable. I had once run fifty miles in just over eight hours. How long could tomorrow take?

Realistically, fifty miles might take a very long time. From the Lansing Manor Visitor's Center, where I had arrived early this morning, I had progressed twenty-three miles, but it had taken all day. My speed—if that was the right word to describe the limping progress—was inexplicably slow, barely above one mile per hour. Maybe the nap by the church in West Conesville had lasted longer than I realized. In any case, this pace was, as feared, even worse than it had been in the Catskills.

I studied my feet. The blisters had worsened and needed to be drained and rebandaged. My left calf looked okay, but it was tender to the touch. Below it, the ankle was swollen and beginning to bruise.

Fortunately, I now had some help. Not only had Cheryl provided a respite from the storm, but Sue would be here tomorrow to help get me through the day. To finish the Long Path, I'd take all the help I could get. I would definitely need it.

I went to sleep listening to thunder rolling through town and rain beating on the roof. For now, I was warm and dry. But tomorrow the trail would be soaked.

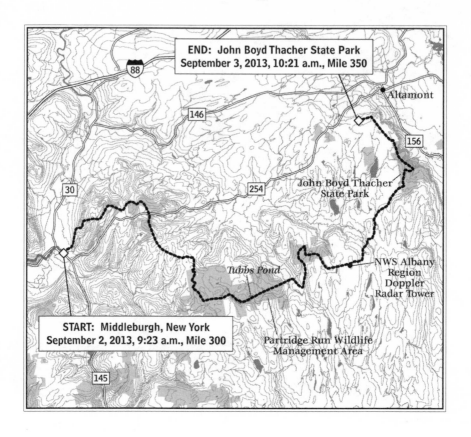

END: John Boyd Thacher State Park
September 3, 2013, 10:21 a.m., Mile 350

88

Altamont

146

156

30

254

John Boyd Thacher
State Park

Tubbs Pond

NWS Albany
Region
Doppler
Radar Tower

START: Middleburgh, New York
September 2, 2013, 9:23 a.m., Mile 300

Partridge Run Wildlife
Management Area

145

Chapter 11

Confronting Zeno's Paradox

To see nothing anywhere but what you may reach it and pass it,
To conceive no time, however distant, but what you may reach
  it and pass it,
To look up or down no road but it stretches and waits for you

                    —Walt Whitman, "Song of the Open Road"

The joy of moving and surmounting, of attrition and progression,
the thirst for space, for miles and leagues of distance, for sights and
prospects, to cross mountains and thread rivers, and defy frost, heat,
snow, danger, difficulties. . . . from that day forth [you are] enrolled
in the noble army of walkers.

              —John Burroughs, "The Exhilarations of the Road"

Middleburgh, New York, Monday, September 2, 2013, 9:23 a.m.

The first thing I discovered upon waking and rolling out of bed was that
my feet were swollen and tender. I tottered around packing up gear, trying to walk on the outside edges rather than the balls of my feet.

At around 8:30 a.m. Drew got back from the late shift at his job.
We had a couple of minutes to catch up before Sue showed up in the
family SUV, with Odie riding shotgun as he likes to do. It was a beautiful
August morning, and the three of us would have enjoyed hanging out

together and talking about life, but the clock was ticking, and I needed to be moving. Sue and I quickly drew up a plan, and then I was hobbling down the street, leaning on the poles, trying to get some blood flowing through painful feet.

The Long Path followed a street for about a mile, then turned onto a steep trail that climbed four hundred feet up a rocky escarpment, in some places at a 45-degree angle, or so it seemed. With my ankle swollen and inflexible, it was difficult going. I turned out the left foot, stepped forward tentatively with the right, dug in with the trekking polls, and in this manner struggled up the slope one step at a time, all the while trying to keep from sliding down backward.

According to the notes, somewhere along the escarpment there grew ancient red cedars, some more than five hundred years old. I looked up at the largest, tallest trees growing on the slope, searching for clues to their age. Afterward I read that the oldest trees grew in poor soil among clefts in the rocks and were stunted, twisted, and gnarled, not tall and stately. They had survived precisely because they went unnoticed, otherwise they would long ago have been harvested for timber. And they survived because they didn't give up. Researchers found one tree that had been blown down twice, but each time its stubborn root system sent up a shoot that grew into a new trunk. One specimen, now dead, was estimated to have reached 614 years in age. It would have first sprouted as a tiny sapling in the fourteenth century and would have already been five hundred years old when the Catskill Mountain House, America's first resort, was built in 1823.

The path squeezed through a split in the cliffs, and I pulled myself up and through, poles dangling from wrist straps and rattling against the rocks. From the top of the escarpment, I turned around to catch the view across the Schoharie Valley. Earlier in the summer, I had looked across the broad valley, admired the streets of Middleburgh laid out below, and peered at Vrooman's Nose in the distance. But this morning, in the time it had taken me to reach this spot, the sky had clouded over, and the vista was now blocked by mist.

On a positive note, the top of the escarpment was flat, and I made a little better time now as the path followed old forest roads. After a bit, the trail turned onto a rough footpath through the woods and crossed a series of streams.

Having reached these hills, I was now in the former territory of the Mohicans, an Eastern Algonquian tribe of Native Americans who had lived in the valleys of the Hudson, Mohawk, and Hoosic Rivers. Mohican territory was bounded on the west by Schoharie Creek, which the bridge into Middleburgh now crosses, and on the south by the Catskill Creek, whose source lay somewhere below the escarpment I had just climbed. As I stumbled along the trail, I thought back to the film, *The Last of the Mohicans*, and the image of Daniel Day-Lewis, running silently through the forest. Well, here I was finally acting out my fantasy.

To be honest, the inspiration for the fantasy wasn't particularly authentic. Day-Lewis is not a Native American—he's British. Furthermore, the character he played, Hawkeye, wasn't a Mohican, but a white man who had been adopted into the Mohican tribe. The film was shot in North Carolina, not New York.

When they first encountered the Dutch in 1609, the Mohicans numbered about eight thousand. A hundred years later, after the devastating impact of European diseases, their numbers had dwindled to around eight hundred, a decline of 90 percent. Pressured by constant war with their Iroquois rivals, the Mohawks, then pushed out of their lands by European traders and colonists, the Mohicans retreated west, eventually settling in Wisconsin. Remarkably, the tribe persevered, and today some fifteen hundred members live in the Stockbridge-Munsee Community Band of Mohican Indians, a reservation in Wisconsin, where they have created a museum, library, and online resources to preserve their heritage. The community website displays a special design that means "Many Trails" and symbolizes endurance, strength, and hope.

Something about the Mohicans had inspired James Fenimore Cooper. He saw in them, or imagined he saw, a vitality and connection with nature that Europeans no longer enjoyed. He described the

Mohicans as "children of the woods": stoic, seemingly unaffected by fatigue, they walked with a "free air and proud carriage" and spoke in voices that were "soft and musical." Those who had not been corrupted by the white man's ways, especially liquor, displayed the "noblest proportions of man," as if they were "some precious relic of the Grecian chisel."

Cooper published his novel in 1826. The book went on to capture the imagination of millions of readers. One hundred sixty-six years later, a Hollywood producer created the movie, and the opening scene stirred something in me. Now some twenty years later I found myself moving through former Mohican lands.

What would a seventeenth-century Mohican brave have thought of me, limping through the forest with the aid of ultralight carbon trekking poles? It would be hard to say. Yet some kind of spark had leapt across the gap between then and now.

∾

About an hour later, the path emerged onto a dirt road where Sue and Odie were waiting. Sue reported that a family of young piglets and their large mom had wandered by. We debated whether their owners trusted them to range across the countryside unsupervised, or whether they had escaped and were now feral.

She showed me a picture she had taken on her phone. "They don't look feral," I said. On the contrary, the piglets looked freshly bathed and well-mannered. "They look like they're just out for a stroll."

"The mom wasn't friendly," Sue responded. "She gave me the once-over and indicated I should keep my distance." Odie, she added, had stayed in the car. I kept my mouth shut, but the mother pig's attitude seemed entirely consistent with my observation that the Long Path was used mostly by animals, some of whom acted as if they owned the trail.

(Sue dutifully reported the incident to the Department of Environmental Conservation, which regards feral pigs as a growing problem and acknowledges it has had difficulty capturing the wily animals.)

Sue had brought an enormous quantity of food, and I gorged myself on watermelon, mango, and apples. Happily refueled, I marched out onto the next section of the trail. After a couple of hours, I met Sue again. This time, instead of eating, I took off my shoes and checked my feet. My socks were low cut, and with my feet swollen, the skin was beginning to chafe against the lip of the shoe, right below the ankles. Dirt and debris had accumulated in the fabric, adding to the irritation. I asked Sue if she would scout for some new socks before the next resupply.

It was now early afternoon. I had made some progress, but there were still nearly forty miles to go. There was no time to stop. As I limped off, it occurred to me that I'd forgotten to eat anything and had merely pocketed a couple of small apples. I'd have to make up the calories at the next resupply, I thought to myself unhappily, recognizing that this wasn't the first time I had made this mistake.

The path followed a paved road, and I moved forward, sometimes power-walking, sometimes trotting very slowly, and eventually arrived at the entrance to the Partridge Run Wildlife Management Area. This was new territory. I hoped it would be an easy trail, allowing me to make up some time. However, those hopes were soon dashed. The path followed a snowmobile trail, and while it might have gotten a lot of use during the winter, there was no one out here now, and the trail was overgrown. It's hard to run through knee-high grass even when you're feeling strong, because you can't see where your feet are landing. In my current condition, running through grass wasn't an option. I plowed forward into a section of the trail with waist-high wildflowers, feeling increasingly frustrated and sour.

I just couldn't seem to get a break, I groaned to myself. After the Catskills, the path was supposed to get easier—at least that had been the hope—but instead things had gone from bad to worse.

With some alarm, I recalled Zeno's paradox, the thought problem posed by an ancient Greek philosopher, Zeno of Elea (490–430 BC). According to the paradox, an arrow can never reach its target, because before it can do so, it must first reach the halfway point. And before it can reach the halfway point, it must cover half that distance. And before it can cover half that distance, it must cover half of that, and so on. Even though I was nearing the finish of the Long Path, with every mile I covered, my pace was slowing, and the time of arrival was stretching out further and further. From seven days to eight, and now, I realized with alarm, it might take nine. Or longer. I pictured myself within a few miles of the finish, lying on the ground curled up in a fetal position.

While anything short of twelve days would establish a new record, I didn't have twelve days. I needed to be back at work.

Feeling first angry, then tired and confused, I pushed forward through the tall wildflowers until the trail finally entered the woods, where the path was mercifully clear of vegetation.

But conditions soon deteriorated again. The path reemerged from the woods and rejoined the snowmobile trail, and now I was once again fighting through waist-high wildflowers. I caught sight of a three-pronged branch lying on the ground. It seemed strangely familiar. Then I saw a sign, which indicated a road, which sounded a lot like the road I had first arrived on. Well, maybe the trail rejoined that road, I thought to myself hopefully. I stopped, pulled out the notes, and, heart sinking, tried to figure out where I was, but the landmarks were unclear. I kept moving forward and sure enough, soon arrived back at the entrance to Partridge Run. I had gotten turned around.

At least the situation was now clear, and I knew where to go. Self-pity gone, I faced about and marched purposefully through the wild-flowers for the third time. Once in the woods again, I exercised extreme diligence to locate and follow each blaze. This time I avoided whatever had confused me before and in due course found myself crossing a paved road again.

The next linkup with Sue was to be at a place called Tubbs Pond. Surely this was it. Out came the notes, and the commentary seemed consistent with the fact that I had just crossed a paved road. I called Sue on the phone. She was still en route. I said I'd wait for her here and sat down on the ground and relaxed a bit, enjoying the watery afternoon sunlight and admiring fields of tall grass waving in the wind.

But something didn't feel right. If I had indeed made it to Tubbs Pond, then surely a body of water would be visible, but as I looked about, there was nothing in sight but fields. Out came the course notes. It now appeared that Tubbs Pond lay a couple of miles further along. In my eagerness to arrive at the next linkup, my mind had raced ahead, like a horse whose rider has dropped the reins, interpreting the directions as corresponding to where I *wanted* to be, not where I *was*. I pulled myself wearily back to my feet and limped on.

The next two miles went by in a blur. The trail wound through pleasant woods and fields, but there were no people. Why would anyone venture out this way? There were no mountains, no views, no reservoirs, no waterfalls, no towns, not even a graveyard. It was a fine enough place to scoot around on a snowmobile, but there was nothing notable to attract hikers. It suddenly occurred to me I hadn't seen a single hiker since the Catskills, almost seventy-five miles ago.

I finally linked up with Sue and loaded my pack with food. She had found some new socks, and I changed into a fresh pair. This was to be my last resupply. Tomorrow was Tuesday, and she had to be at work. Sue got back in the SUV and buckled the seatbelt. Odie jumped onto the passenger seat and gave me a quizzical glance. I waved as they drove off.

There was plenty of time to make it to the end, but I was moving very slowly. Here it was late afternoon, and I had been walking all day yet had barely covered twenty-five miles, not much better than two miles per hour. The next twenty-five would probably be even slower, as it would be dark. In regard to one section, the notes indicated that "there has been recent logging activity in this area and the trail may be hard to follow." Needless to say, this sentence was not reassuring.

I pictured an arrow following a parabolic arc toward its target, velocity slowing. Soon it is hanging in the air, motionless.

The sun set. I was moving through shadows, and then it became dark. The notes referenced beaver ponds, stands of spruce, views of the Catskills—all invisible in the gloom.

Somehow the blazes took me through the recently logged area without issue. Emerging onto Woodstock Road, I perked up a little. Now there were twenty miles to go. I began to feel just a little bit excited, although with a swollen ankle, strained calf, and blistered feet, my pace remained sluggish. Twenty miles could still take a really long time.

According to the notes, this road led to the National Weather Service Albany Region Doppler Radar Tower. This sounded like an important facility with antennae and rotating radar dishes, and people inside tracking dangerous storms—it was something interesting to aim for. I strode forward on the pavement, eager to reach this objective and see what it was all about.

After a few minutes, the blazes turned off onto a gravel road, which led to a small, squat, featureless building. I played the flashlight across its walls, but there was nothing to see. There was no sign of activity, no radar dish, not even windows. My spirits sank a notch. But the next section would be downhill, and when I reached the valley floor, there would be only seventeen miles left.

Seventeen miles!

On a downhill slope, I could pick up the pace, cover some distance, start to tick off the remaining miles.

The blazes took me through what seemed like a tunnel between trees. My flashlight flickered out. I turned on the headlamp. Its batteries were low. In the dim light I stumbled on rocks and splashed into puddles. But I wouldn't stop—not with seventeen miles to go. But I couldn't run, either—my ankle wouldn't flex at all. I tried to scoot forward, taking a running step with my right leg, then swinging my left leg forward while I leaned on the poles. I tried skipping. An image came to mind of Groucho Marx scuttling around, cigar clenched in his teeth and hands clasped behind his back. I could do that, I thought. But the truth was, even a slow stumbling walk was becoming difficult. And now the chafing on my feet began to sting. It felt like needles were being stuck into my skin just below the ankles. I started to curse under my breath. I thought there were lights around me—surely the trail was cutting behind someone's house. I began to curse out loud, partly in irritation, and partly with the secret hope that someone might hear me and come to the rescue. I was supposed to be running down this trail, picking up speed, saving time, and ticking off the miles. But instead I was barely moving. And now I was shouting with pain and frustration.

From somewhere in the depths of my mind, a quiet little voice piped up: "Stop. If it's not working, you've got to stop and fix it."

Oh, but I didn't want to stop. I didn't want to sit on the wet ground. I didn't want to untie my shoes and take them off. I didn't want to fuss around with the blister kit. More than anything else, I didn't want to stop moving, because I just wanted to get the Long Path over and done with.

People sometimes think that to complete an ultramarathon requires discipline, as if you had to bark at yourself like a drill sergeant, willing yourself to keep marching when all you want to do is lie down. But that's not right. What keeps you going is the goal you've committed yourself to and the thrill that you know will come from completing a tough challenge. Discipline is something different. It's the act of sticking to plan, which may require you to stop and fix a problem even though you'd rather keep moving. There had been some notable gaps in my self-discipline during this journey, for example, the numerous times when I failed to stop and adequately replenish calories.

It was no use arguing. The voice was right. With a sigh, I stopped, found a patch of damp ground to sit on, and unpacked my kit. To start with, I put new batteries in the headlamp and flashlight and was rewarded with a burst of brilliant light. Then I untied shoes, removed socks, and wrung out water. Bending over my feet, I cleaned off the area around my ankles using alcohol swabs. I had to scrub hard, as bits of dirt and pine needles had become embedded in the skin, especially where the swollen ankle had rubbed against the shoe. In some places the chafed skin was red, in other places it was starting to bleed from nicks and scratches. After cleaning the skin as best I could, I rubbed on disinfectant, applied cotton patches, and taped them in place, carefully circling the tape around my ankle and the bottom of my foot hoping that the tape wouldn't create new blisters. The bandages on the balls of my feet were still intact, so I left them alone.

Gritting my teeth, I pulled on the dirty, damp socks and then wedged my feet back into the shoes, which were still soaked. Leaning on the poles, I levered myself back up to my feet and took a few tentative steps. This was not good, but it was better than before. I limped off down the hill. After some period of time the trail emerged onto a field of wet grass, which thoroughly soaked my shoes and socks once again.

I was walking past a house, shining my light on the trees around me, looking for the next blaze, when suddenly a hostile shout rang out.

"Hey! What are you doing out there?"

A man was standing in the door of the house. I couldn't see much, but from the tone of his voice, if he had a shotgun, it was leveled right at my midsection. It was around 4:00 a.m., and a homeowner might well be suspicious of a stranger prowling around his backyard at this time of night.

"I'm following the Long Path" I shouted back, trying to sound legitimate, "I'm going to set a new record!"

The man relaxed. "Well it goes about a thousand feet up the hill," he yelled back. "Sorry to shout. We don't see many hikers around here." That was hardly a surprise.

Just as he had indicated, the trail led uphill and then jumped through a gap in the bushes leading to yet another alley between a cornfield and a hedgerow. The path was soft and uneven, and I stepped forward tentatively. But my spirits were rising. I was making progress again. I was now within fifteen miles of the finish.

Getting to the end of this adventure was starting to seem very real, and for a moment I choked up as I imagined reaching the finish. I thought back to the points where I had almost given up: the blaze

I couldn't find without Todd's help, the struggle to reach Nickerson's Campground, the thunderstorm on the mountain.

My reverie was soon interrupted as I looked up and saw two beady eyes reflected in the beam of the light. The eyes belonged to a small black animal with a white stripe down its back and a bushy tail. A moment ago, the skunk had been burrowing in the soft earth. I didn't know what it hoped to find, but it was happily engaged in its work. When it looked up and saw me, the smile dropped from its face.

I took a step back. The skunk gave me an unfriendly glance, but didn't budge.

With the finish line almost in sight, I was eager to keep moving. But getting sprayed by a skunk didn't seem like an appealing way to finish—especially since I was hoping for a TV interview and didn't want to make a poor impression. After nine days on the trail, I surely smelled bad enough already.

Theodore Roosevelt once said, "In any moment of decision, the best thing you can do is the right thing, the next best thing is the wrong thing, and the worst thing you can do is nothing." Well, clearly I needed to do something.

With some trepidation, I picked up a small rock and tossed it at the skunk, not wanting to hit the animal, but thinking the rock might persuade it to look for a different hole somewhere else. The rock landed with a soft thud. The skunk looked up from its hole, its expression hostile. It sized me up and evidently unimpressed, returned to its digging.

I picked up a heavier rock, and tossed it a little bit closer to the defiant animal. The skunk looked up again and this time appeared to make some sort of mental calculation, weighing alternatives. Visibly irritated, it ceded its ground and ambled slowly off among the cornstalks, but not without a final glance in my direction that seemed to say, "Better watch your back."

I stepped forward cautiously, shining my light on full power into the cornfield, on guard against a possible ambush from the flank.

And soon I was back on a paved road, with only ten miles to go. Now my spirits were really soaring. Blinking back tears of excitement, I began to run—ankle, calf, blistered and chafed feet all but forgotten. After so many miles of struggling through grass and weeds, tripping on rocks, scrambling up steep slopes, the pavement felt fast, like running a marathon. I've done it, I thought to myself. For the first time in my life, I will have set a record.

The road reached an intersection, and I began counting steps to ensure I wouldn't miss the turnoff into the John Boyd Thacher State Park. And soon enough, in the morning's first light, I saw a Long Path disk nailed to a thin birch tree. Aqua blazes pointed the way straight into the forest.

I had arrived at the monster's lair. The Long Path had used up its bag of tricks. It now lay defenseless. There was nothing but seven miles between me and victory.

The TV station was expecting me to arrive at the finish just before noon. Now I called them and revised the ETA to midmorning.

I headed into the woods, jogging along happily as the path meandered through a forest of beech, birch, and maple, feeling enormously excited. After a couple of miles, I emerged onto the Helderberg Escarpment—and it took my breath away. Standing on an observation platform above a line of cliffs, I could see all the way to the Hudson River in the east. Albany was a cluster of buildings about ten miles distant. To the north stood the Adirondacks and the mountains of Vermont. Low clouds scudded across the landscape, looking like smoke upon a battlefield.

With five miles left to go, I paused to eat breakfast, mixing water into a packet of freeze-dried lasagna. It was unappealing, even in my weakened state, especially the dry sections where the water had not fully penetrated. I stirred it up some more and spooned down as much as I could tolerate. I looked up again at the distant mountains and lowering sky.

Only five miles left to go.

Of course, before I could get there, I'd have to make it two-and-a-half miles to the halfway point, and before that, I'd need to cover the next mile and a quarter. But that all seemed within the realm of the possible.

I walked along the cliffs admiring the views until the trail headed back into the woods. I trotted along slowly, figuring there were about two miles to go. But then I saw a sign that read three-and-a-half.

My energy crashed. Three-and-a-half miles suddenly seemed like an enormous distance. I slowed to a walk. But the TV crew would be waiting. It was time to run, time to get this over and done with.

But I felt so listless. I stopped for a moment, pulled out the rest of the lasagna, and finished it off.

I tried to run, but I couldn't. My energy was gone; I felt deeply lethargic. I needed more calories. My sprint along the paved road must have exhausted my remaining reserves. I pulled out the last bag of dried fruit and nuts and chomped on them listlessly.

I tried again to run, but still I couldn't. It seemed I could barely move one foot in front of the other. I recalled feeling sluggish like this earlier on the trail, and how the jolt of a thousand calories of chocolate had reignited the engine. Now I reached into a pouch on my belt, pulled out a chocolate bar, and ate as much of it as I could. It was tasteless. I couldn't finish it. Nothing happened.

My phone rang. I ignored it. Looking down at my watch, it was clear I wouldn't make the finish time I had confidently projected just a little while earlier.

The phone rang again. Suppressing my irritation, I answered it and told the station that I was only one mile out, although it was probably closer to two-and-a-half.

I tried to pick up a trot. But I couldn't. No matter what I ate, it was like throwing food into a bottomless hole. There was no response from my body. It was out of juice and unwilling to dip any further into dwindling stocks.

"So you have one last surprise for me," I snarled at the forest, imagining that the spirit of the Long Path was toying with me, like a cat with a mouse. Maybe Zeno was right, and movement is illusory. Time had slowed to a crawl. It might yet grind to a halt.

A sign indicated 1.5 miles remained. I broke into a slow jog.

I focused on lifting my knees and began to count steps. If I could make it to three hundred steps, that would take out a quarter of a mile, leaving only 1.25 to go.

At some point, half a mile was left, as best I could tell. Zeno be damned. I broke into a run, huffing and puffing.

Two hundred yards away a young woman was standing with a camera mounted on a tripod. I sprinted, as best I could, intent on looking good and finishing strong.

I passed the woman and camera and looked around for the three blazes that would signify the termination of the Long Path. But there were only two blazes, indicating a turn to the right. I followed these onto a paved road and headed downhill at full speed toward a single blaze painted on a telephone pole.

Then I remembered that while the Long Path officially ended here, the blazes continued further north toward its eventual destination in the Adirondacks. I had just run a quarter-mile past the finish, and the Long Path had gotten a final laugh at my expense.

I trudged back up the hill and returned to the parking lot. The young lady from the TV station asked me some questions. I explained about the challenges of the run, then switched gears and talked about the New York Road Runners' Youth Programs and how important it was for young people to get an introduction to health and fitness. I tried to smile and make a good impression, but suddenly in midsentence I felt lightheaded. I sank down to the ground, head in hands, trying to regain my equilibrium. I stood back up and tried to talk a little longer, but had to sit down again. The interview was over.

My friend Lisa was there to drive me to the bus station. She took a picture of me at the end of the Long Path, then escorted me to her car. I climbed in and was immediately unconscious.

Chapter 12

The Long Brown Path Never Ends

One who pressed forward incessantly and never rested from his labors, who grew fast and made infinite demands on life, would always find himself in a new country or wilderness, and surrounded by the raw material of life. He would be climbing over the prostrate stems of primitive forest trees.

—Henry David Thoreau, "Walking"

My run through the Hudson Valley was now over, and when the clock finally stopped ticking, there was a new record for the Long Path: 9 days, 3 hours, and 6 minutes. The run was over, but the experience had generated a kind of momentum that kept pushing me forward, and my journey would continue both on trails and off.

After picking me up at the northern terminus of the Long Path, Lisa took me to breakfast somewhere along the Thruway, where I sat in a daze, poking listlessly at a platter of bacon and eggs. Then she dropped me off at the bus station in New Paltz, a small college town nestled in the shadow of the northern Shawangunks. After purchasing a one-way ticket back to New York City, I lay down in the waiting room and closed my eyes.

I woke up an hour later, famished—so hungry I could barely move. This wasn't a case of a growling stomach, a craving for sweets, a dip in energy, or any of the normal signs of hunger. This was my body in panic mode, as if the spirit of self-preservation had just awakened from a deep sleep, discovered what I'd done, and slammed a red button marked "emergency stop."

Spotting a small deli adjoining the bus station, I staggered over to the counter, braced myself to keep from falling over, and started grabbing rolls from the shelf and biting into them even before the clerk had swiped my card. But the rolls were hard to chew and did nothing to stabilize my energy level. I considered sliding to the floor and waiting for someone to call an ambulance. But I needed to make it home in time for my business trip the next morning, so that option wouldn't work.

Suddenly that image of David Horton eating ice cream during his 2,663-mile run along the Pacific Coast Trail popped back into mind. His crew brought him ice cream because it was the highest-calorie food they could find, and easy to eat. Ice cream suddenly seemed like a very good idea.

The deli had none, but I could see another deli out the window. Mustering my strength, I shuffled across the street.

There was no ice cream here either, but I ordered the next best thing: a blueberry smoothie. And then another one. A little bit of energy flowed back into my veins—just enough to hobble back across the street and board the bus.

The next morning I stepped onto the bathroom scale and found myself down eight pounds or about 5 percent of my previous bodyweight. To be sure, this was a very modest loss of weight compared to what is endured by the many people in the world who don't get enough to eat. But for someone who's been used to three square meals a day, this was a shock to the system.

I stepped off the scale, showered, shaved, buttoned my suit, cinched the belt an extra inch, and hailed a cab for the airport. When I got there, walking through the terminal was an ordeal. My feet were still swollen and chafed and my ankle wouldn't flex. Sitting on the airplane, my feet hurt. On arriving at my destination, I bought a package of bandages and applied them liberally to my ankles and the bottoms of my feet.

On the drive in from the airport, I spotted a fast-food restaurant in the distance and decided to swing by and pick up a sandwich. But the turnoff wasn't clearly marked, and the entrance flashed by in the rearview mirror before I could react. The morning traffic was unforgiving. There was no opportunity to turn around for the next half a mile.

I pounded the steering wheel in frustration, wondering what kind of idiots would site a fast-food restaurant where you can't see the entrance. Reaching a U-turn lane, I yanked the wheel, whipped the poor rental about, then punched the accelerator until smoke poured from the tires, all the while shouting angrily about bad signage. I got my sandwich, as well as two lunches and dinner that day and two dinners the next.

∾

The blisters healed within two or three days and the chafing within four or five. But my feet still hurt. After three weeks, my weight was back to normal, and after a month, my feet no longer bothered me, except for the toes, which continued to tingle for another two months.

Later that fall, on a dark, drizzly night, Sue, Philip, Emeline, and I drove to the tiny town of Palenville for dinner at Fernwood. I thanked Emil for the two glasses of Coke, and he smiled when he remembered my visit.

For a period of time, I dreamed of the trail. A ribbon of brown earth punctuated by rocks gleaming gray and white kept flowing and flowing and flowing beneath my feet.

∾

That same fall, Sue, Odie, and I were headed north for a weekend in the Shawangunks when I pulled off the Palisades Parkway and announced that we were going to visit Letchworth Village Cemetery, the creepy place I had passed through during the first evening of the run, where so many patients had been buried beneath nameless headstones. Sue gave me a skeptical glance, but agreed we could spare twenty minutes. It took a few of those minutes to find the cemetery, but after a little confusion, we pulled into a gravel parking area on the side of the road where, with a shock of recognition, I spotted an aqua blaze painted on a tree. A short path in the woods led us to a small hillock sheltered in a hollow between mountains. And there stood a large, polished monument, which was inscribed along the top:

THOSE WHOSE NAMES SHALL NOT BE FORGOTTEN

Below was a long list of names. Behind the monument, rows of T-shaped markers dotted a grassy slope, looking peaceful in the morning sunlight as if public recognition of the wrongs they had suffered had helped reconcile them with their fate. We read a few of the names, then walked once around the cemetery, huddled up against a cold wind blowing down from the mountains.

Before returning to the Parkway, we drove through the remains of Letchworth Village. I was struck by the massive size of the campus, which totals twenty-three-hundred acres and includes 130 buildings arrayed in neat rows on open lawns.

The project was named for William Pryor Letchworth, a wealthy businessman turned philanthropist. Having tired of the burdens of business, Letchworth retreated to an estate in upstate New York and threw himself into charity work. He accepted a position on the New York State Board of Charities, where as part of his duties he inspected the state's asylums, poorhouses, and juvenile reformatories. Then, at his own expense, he traveled across the United States and Europe to research the plight of epileptics, poor children, and the insane, and based on these experiences he wrote two books with observations and recommendations to improve their care. He died in 1910, the year before the village bearing his name would open.

Despite the huge resources with which it was launched, Letchworth Village was a failure. Today the large campus sits vacant and decaying, one of many failed projects the Long Path had taken me past, including abandoned roads and rail beds, a ditch filled with stagnant water that was once part of the Delaware and Hudson Canal, and the site of the former Catskill Mountain House, once America's finest resort. These were all reminders that the works of man are subject to the laws of growth and decay, no different from the mountains and forests.

While the Long Path taught me lessons in failure and decay, I also witnessed examples of success and growth. I learned about the infrastructure that supports New York City, including the bridges, highways, power lines, and water-supply system. I also began to better appreciate the role of the Trail Conference, the Open Space Institute, and other organizations that have played leadership roles in preserving the natural environment. There is sometimes a tension between preservation and economic improvement, but nonetheless these organizations have done a magnificent job preserving some of the most beautiful areas. They've developed the long-term vision, managed the financial resources, and built consensus around the value of preserved land, both for its inherent beauty and as an economic asset for local communities.

In regards to the Trail Conference, it's fortunate that Robert Moses missed Raymond Torrey with that smoking stand he threw at him. Pugnacious to the end, Moses was unapologetic about the fight, his only regret being that he hadn't been able to "finish that crackpot." Not only did Torrey stand up to Moses, and not only was he instrumental in promoting the Long Path and the Appalachian Trail, his contribution to the Trail Conference was so large that it took an entire committee to get the same work done when he was gone.

Thanks to Torrey's contributions and the work of countless other people, the New York–New Jersey Trail Conference is going strong today, with two thousand volunteers, ten thousand members, and over a hundred thousand affiliated members when you include the local hiking and running clubs with which it is affiliated.

∽

After the run was over, I reflected on a number of lessons learned.

I had originally determined to run the Long Path on a self-supported basis, with success or failure totally dependent on my individual effort. As members of a social species, we all need to find a balance between individual accomplishment and working with others. While I'm generally a team-oriented person, at times I get frustrated with the need to cooperate, collaborate, and accommodate others, especially when it slows me down or makes life complicated.

But while it was my intention to go it alone, the success of the run ended up depending on many people. To start with, I was inspired by David O'Neill, who came up with the idea of running the Long Path in the first place. The companionship of Elaine and her friends helped get me off to a good start on day one. Todd gave me crucial navigational guidance when I was struggling deep in the woods at night and in a rainstorm and couldn't find the next blaze. I benefitted from the kindness of strangers, including Emil at Fernwood and Doug at Nickerson's Campground. Drew and Cheryl put me up in Middleburgh, giving me a much-appreciated respite from the trail before the final push. And my wife Sue saved the day, making two separate trips to resupply me with desperately needed calories. Finally, besides the contributions of friends and family, it's fair to say there wouldn't be a Long Path to run on if it weren't for the staff and volunteers of the Trail Conference, including Long Path cochairmen Andy Garrison and Jakob Franke and all the volunteer supervisors and maintainers who keep the trail clear.

While there were some low points during the nine days, the experience left me even more passionate than before about the sport of ultrarunning. Perhaps you could call me a "green exercise" enthusiast after all. Regardless of what label you prefer, it's not just me: many people find great energy in getting outside and moving through the natural environment, regardless of pace or distance. John Burroughs described the exhilaration of moving in his 1881 essay, "Footpaths":

It is not the walking merely, it is keeping yourself in tune for a walk, in the spiritual and bodily condition in which you can find entertainment and exhilaration in so simple and natural a pastime. You are eligible to any good fortune when you are in the condition to enjoy a walk. When the air and the water taste sweet to you, how much else will taste sweet! When the exercise of your limbs affords you pleasure, and the play of your senses upon the various objects and shows of nature quickens and stimulates your spirit, your relation to the world and to yourself is what it should be,—simple and direct and wholesome. The mood in which you set out on a spring or autumn ramble or a sturdy winter walk, and your greedy feet have to be restrained from devouring the distances too fast, is the mood in which your best thoughts and impulses come to you, or in which you might embark on any noble and heroic enterprise. Life is sweet in such moods, the universe is complete, and there is no failure or imperfection anywhere.

Finally, in reflecting on the experience, it seems that I could learn a trick or two from Walt Whitman. There were points during the run when the pressure of going after a record caused me to make shortsighted decisions (such as skipping on opportunities to get more calories), and there were other times when slow progress made me extremely frustrated (for example, in the cornfield outside Middleburgh). Perhaps I could learn to be a little more of a "loafer," that is, to operate more patiently, with a little more held in reserve. If you understand the path you're traveling, Whitman seems to say, then just be patient, you'll make progress in the right direction sooner or later:

Not I, not anyone else can travel that road for you,
You must travel it yourself.

It is not far, it is within reach,
Perhaps you have been on it since you were born and
    did not know . . .

❧

The Long Path took me past seven cemeteries (as best I remember), a reminder that all of our paths end at the same place sooner or later.

Whitman died in 1892 at age seventy-two. As he was lying on his deathbed, John Burroughs came to check on his friend and mentor. Whitman looked up at him and said, "It's all right, John, it's all right."

In *Song of Myself*, he had written, "Has anyone supposed it lucky to be born? / I hasten to inform him or her it is just as lucky to die, and I know it."

After losing a bid for a third term as president, Theodore Roosevelt undertook a journey to the Amazon and decided, at the urging of a Brazilian army officer, to explore an uncharted river. During the trip, he suffered from lack of food, badly injured his leg, and nearly died from infection. Weakened from the ordeal, he passed away five years later in 1919 at age sixty. He not only talked about the "strenuous life," he lived it to the end. Upon learning of his death, Burroughs wrote in his journal: "I love him more than I thought I did . . . and I remember his great kindness to me personally."

In reading about Burroughs's life, I discovered to my surprise that he worked for several years as a bank examiner for the U.S. Treasury. He was good at his job, but it required constant travel, and he longed to spend more time in his beloved Catskills. He eventually left this job, bought land on the Hudson, and took up farming, while also devoting himself to his writing.

Burroughs died in 1921 just short of his eighty-fourth birthday while riding a train back to the Catskills from a vacation in California. His last words: "How far are we from home?"

∾

One day an email arrived from the Trail Conference, announcing that a project was under way to relocate the Long Path outside Phoenicia from the roads to the woods. On a whim, I asked my son Philip if he'd like to spend a day working on a trail crew. It would be a chance to get him out in nature and help him see with his own eyes the role volunteers play, rather than listening to me lecture on the subject.

To my surprise, he looked up and replied, "Sure Dad," his face lighting up, and a sparkle in his eyes.

A few weeks later we pulled into a gravel parking area near Phoenicia, got out of the car, and introduced ourselves to Andy and Jakob.

It had been raining for much of the day, and the trees had lost most of their leaves. After hiking into the forest, Philip and I stood by and watched as Andy and another volunteer wrestled with heavy steel bars, maneuvering a small boulder that blocked the new trail. Andy stepped back for a moment, while Jakob attacked with a pickaxe, loosening dirt and small stones. The rock was soon loose enough to be rotated into position to serve as a perfect step.

Philip and I walked down the trail and looked for a task consistent with our limited trail-building skills. We found a small depression in the path, gathered some flat rocks, smashed them with a sledgehammer, filled the depression with the crushed rock, and covered the crush with dirt. We spent the rest of the day in similar tasks. Our contribution was modest, but we were pleased to have done something useful for the project.

As we were getting ready to hike back to the car, I stepped back for a moment and surveyed the newly created path. My eyes followed the long brown ribbon of fresh earth as it wound its way artfully around a rock ledge, hopped up a series of stone steps, and reached for the spine of the ridge.

When finished, this would be a fine trail. Just looking at it would make you want to run.

Epilogue

A year later, I was trotting along a country road in upstate New York, a road I had run on many times before, close to the spot where I had met the fifty-year-old who had inspired me to seek out my first ultramarathon. The asphalt climbed uphill, passed an occasional ramshackle dwelling, then dropped down a long slope. To the right grew a stand of shagbark hickory trees, the bark peeling from the trunks in long ribbons.

Suddenly, on a telephone pole, I caught sight of a faded aqua blaze. I stopped and rubbed my eyes. An effort had been made to scratch it out or paint it over, but the blaze was still visible. It was unmistakably a Long Path blaze.

A half-mile later, I saw a second blaze.

Looking up at the cliffs of the Shawangunks, I recalled that it was only in the 1980s that the Open Space Institute began purchasing the land to create Sam's Point Preserve, the state park high on the ridge where I had once watched clouds blowing across the moon. Prior to that date, the Long Path must have followed the roads.

In a sense, I had been running on the Long Path for years and never knew it.

Notes and References

Throughout the book, I have made liberal use of the New York–New Jersey Trail Conference's excellent notes for the Long Path, available on the their website at www.nynjtc.org under the heading "Long Path Guide electronic edition."

Chapter 1

A list of Long Path end-to-enders is available on the Trail Conference's website, and statistics on completions of the Appalachian Trail are maintained by the Appalachian Trail Conservancy on its website www.appalachiantrail.org.

For the story of Rick Rescorla, see James B. Stewart, "The Real Heroes Are Dead: A Love Story," *The New Yorker*, February 11, 2002.

Roosevelt's opinions on moral character were published in *The Outlook*, March 31, 1900.

Scott Jurek and Steve Friedman, *Eat and Run: My Unlikely Journey to Ultramarathon Greatness* (New York: Mariner Books, 2013).

Vanessa Runs, *The Summit Seeker: Memoirs of a Trail-Running Nomad* (Y42K Publishing Services, 2013).

Richard Louv's book, *The Nature Principle: Reconnecting with Life in a Virtual Age* (Chapel Hill, NC: Algonquin Books, 2012) provides a summary of research in "green care" and "green exercise."

Henry David Thoreau, *Walden, or a Life in the Woods,* 1854. The quotation on wildness is from the chapter, "Spring," p. 242.

David O'Neill ran a slightly different version of the Long Path that totaled 369 miles.

My first marathon training plans came from Jeff Galloway, *Galloway's Book on Running* (Bolinas, CA: Shelter Publications, 1984).

Frank Giannino's story is told in "Trans-America running bond," *Times Herald Record,* September 14, 2008.

You can read Marshall Ulrich's story in his book, *Running on Empty: An Ultramarathoner's Story of Love, Loss, and a Record-Setting Run Across America* (New York: Avery, 2011).

Chapter 2

A website known simply as "Fastest Known Time" is the most popular site for recording and discussing fastest-known times (www.fastestknown-time.probards.com). Jennifer Pharr Davis's record is listed under the tab for the Appalachian Trail. Of note, during 2015, Scott Jurek beat Jennifer Pharr Davis's time by just a few hours.

I enjoyed Jennifer Pharr Davis's account of her record-setting journey, *Called Again: A Story of Love and Triumph* (New York: Beaufort Books, 2013).

The Devil's Path is one of the eight most dangerous trails in the United States, according to the Sierra Club. More info at "6 of America's Most Dangerous Hiking Trails," *Sierra,* April 11, 2013.

David Horton's record is noted on the Fastest-Known Time website under the tab for "Pacific Crest Trail."

There is indeed uncertainty surrounding the estimation of calories in food. Calorie estimates for food are based largely on a hundred-year old system that relies on the amount of fat, protein, and carbohydrates contained in the food, without allowance for differences in digestibility.

Also, there are enormous variations in how individuals digest and absorb calories, which cannot of course be represented on a label.

My estimate of a hundred calories per mile comes from wearing sports watches with heart-rate monitors, which use algorithms for estimating calories burned as a function of weight, age, and heart rate. While there is a relationship between heart rate and calorie burn, it is imprecise due to many factors, including differences between upper and lower body exercise, temperature, emotions, duration of exercise, and of course individual variations. The most accurate way to estimate calories burned is with lab equipment that measures oxygen consumption. R. A Robergs and L. Kravitz, "Making Sense of Calorie-burning Claims," *IDEA Today* 12, no. 8: 27–32.

Dean Karnazes, *Ultra Marathon Man: Confessions of an All-Night Runner* (New York: Jeremy P. Tarcher/Penguin, 2005).

The Catskill weather summary is from Edward G. Henry, *Catskill Trails: A Ranger's Guide to the High Peaks, Book One—The Northern Catskills* (Delmar, NY: Black Dome Press, 2000), 19.

Thoreau's observations are from *Walden*, 26, 129.

You can watch the opening scenes of the 1992 movie *The Last of the Mohicans* on YouTube, accessed December 15, 2015 at http://www.youtube.com/watch?v=omkIwWGYfWQ.

The etiquette for setting fastest-known times is attributed to runner and adventurer Buzz Burrell and is available on the Fastest-Known Time website under the thread "read first."

Information on the New York Road Runners Youth Services Programs is available at http://www.nyrr.org/youth-and-schools.

Statistics on overweight youth and diabetes prevalence are compiled by the Centers for Disease Control and available on their website, www.cdc.gov.

You can watch a video I made of a NYRR Youth Jamboree that includes the interview with the coaches of the Bronx Zodiacs on YouTube at http://www.youtube.com/watch?v=TOpOp0JkmfI.

Theodore Roosevelt gave his speech, "The Strenuous Life," at the Hamilton Club in Chicago on April 10, 1899.

Chapter 3

For stats on the George Washington Bridge, see the Port Authority of New York and New Jersey's website, www.panynj.gov, under the tab for bridges and tunnels.

For examples of recent research on the health costs associated with commuting, see Jane E. Brody, "Commuting's Hidden Cost," *The New York Times*, October 28, 2013.

The story of the State of New Jersey Federation of Women's Clubs is available on the Palisades Interstate Park Commission's New Jersey website, www.njpalisades.org, under the heading "A Stop along the Long Path."

The Roosevelt quote is from State of New York, *Public Papers of Theodore Roosevelt, Governor* (Albany: Brandow Printing Company, 1900) accessed December 15, 2015, at https://archive.org/stream/publicpapersthe00roosgoog#page/n6/mode/2up.

Whitman's burial house is described in Justin Kaplan, *Walt Whitman: A Life* (New York: Simon and Schuster, 1980), 49–52.

Stats on the Thruway are available on its website, www.thruway.ny.gov.

For a discussion of the Letchworth Village Cemetery, see Peter Applebome, "Giving Names to Souls Forgotten No Longer," *The New York Times*, December 13, 2007.

Chapter 4

The ice sheet is called the Laurentide Ice Sheet, and it must have been several thousand feet thick in the Hudson Valley, as it covered not only

Harriman, but also the Shawangunk Mountains and most of the Catskills. Robert and Johanna Titus, *The Hudson Valley in the Ice Age: A Geological History & Tour* (Delmar, NY: Black Dome Press, 2012), 20–21.

Quotations and commentary on Whitman are from Kaplan, *Walt Whitman*, 12, 21, 83, 90, 104, 107, 318.

The crowd estimate for Times Square is from "Times Square Hosts Record Crowds, Surprise Kisses, and a Big Cleanup," *Associated Press/ NBC New York*, January 1, 2012.

Torrey's 1934 articles with descriptions of the Long Path are maintained on the New York–New Jersey Trail Conference's website, www.nynjtc.org, accessed December 16, 2015, at http://www.nynjtc.org/files/ documents/LBP.pdf.

The fight scene is from Robert A. Caro, *The Power Broker: Robert Moses and the Fall of New York* (New York: Vintage Books, 1974), 317–18; Moses as an old man, 1162.

The story of Rose's Rangers is from Alf Evers, *The Catskills: From Wilderness to Woodstock* (Garden City, NY: Doubleday & Company, 1972), 147–56.

Major Robert Rogers's Standing Orders are available on the U.S. Army's website, www.goarmy.com, accessed December 15, 2015 at http:// www.goarmy.com/ranger/heritage/rodgers-orders.html.

The black-earth regions of the Wallkill Valley are referred to by geologists as "drowned lands." Titus, *The Hudson Valley in the Ice Age*, 58–59, 174–76.

The description of Roosevelt's hunting experience from Edmund Morris, *The Rise of Theodore Roosevelt* (New York: Modern Library, 2010).

Chapter 5

The Basha Kill Area Association provides information on the Basha Kill on its website www.thebashakill.org.

History of Delaware and Hudson Canal from Larry Lowenthal, *From the Coalfields to the Hudson: A History of the Delaware & Hudson Canal* (Fleischmanns, NY: Purple Mountain Press, 1997), 22, 62, 64, 124, 130, 176, 203, 213, 267, 275.

Thoreau's observation of the spotted salamander is from *Walden*, 119.

For an introduction to the geography of the Shawangunk Ridgeline, see Jack Fagan, *Scenes and Walks in the Northern Shawangunks* (Mahwah, NJ: New York–New Jersey Trail Conference, 1998).

A summary of the OSI's vision for the Shawangunks is available on their website, www.osiny.org, accessed December 16, 2015 at http://www.osiny.org/site/PageServer?pagename=places_secondary_Shawangunks&AddInterest=1144.

Robert Anderberg, general counsel of the OSI, is credited with the vision to protect the Gunks. You can read about his story in Tom Butler and Antonio Vizcaino, *Wildlands Philanthropy: The Great American Tradition* (San Rafael, CA: Earth Aware Editions, 2010), 17879.

For a recent update on the OSI's preservation activities, see Lisa W. Foderaro, "Conservation Group Keeps Buying Land, Helping State Parks Grow," *The New York Times*, November 15, 2013.

Chapter 6

David O'Neill's observation was reported in the *Poughkeepsie Journal*, "Runner goes the distance to raise funds for Long Path."

The Nature Conservancy describes its rationale for identifying the Shawangunks as "one of Earth's last great places" on its website, www.nature.org, accessed December 16, 2015, at http://www.nature.org/ourinitiatives/regions/northamerica/unitedstates/newyork/placesweprotect/easternnewyork/wherewework/eastern-shawangunk-mountains.xml.

Views from High Point are from Marc B. Fried, *Shawangunk: Adventure, Exploration, History and Epiphany from a Mountain Wilderness* (Utica, NY: North Country Books, 1998), 12–18.

The Catskill river delta and Acadians are described in Robert Titus, *The Other Side of Time: Essays by "The Catskill Geologist"* (Fleischmanns, NY: Purple Mountain Press, 2007), 80–90.

The National Parks Service has a useful article on the Delaware and Hudson Canal on its website, www.nps.gov, under the category "Upper Delaware."

Chapter 7

Comments on Thoreau are from John Burroughs, "Henry D. Thoreau," *The Century*, July 1882.

Camping trips with Henry Ford, Thomas Edison, and Harvey Firestone, the relationship with Roosevelt, and the impact on conservation are from Edward Kanze, *The World of John Burroughs*, (New York: Harry N. Abrams, 1993), 77, 110, 142. Burroughs described the trip to Yellowstone in *Camping & Tramping with Roosevelt* (New York: Houghton, Mifflin, 1906), and Roosevelt included his account in *Outdoor Pastimes of an American Hunter*, (New York: C. Scribner's Sons, 1905). Burroughs's description of Whitman and his poetry, the trip to Alaska, and the hiking and bird-counting trip with Roosevelt are from Edward J. Renehan, Jr., *John Burroughs: An American Naturalist* (Post Mills, VT: Chelsea Green Publishing Company, 1992), 208, 223, 250, 255, 260. Also see Kaplan, *Walt Whitman*, 307.

The video *A Day in the Life of John Burroughs* is available on YouTube, accessed December 16, 2015, at http://www.youtube.com/watch?v=3EftVouZ5Qg.

Burroughs's account of climbing Slide Mountain is from "The Heart of the Southern Catskills," in *In The Catskills: Selections from the Writings of John Burroughs* (New York: Houghton Mifflin Company, 1910).

Comments on Burroughs's penchant for manual labor from H. A. Haring, ed., *The Slabsides Book of John Burroughs* (New York: Houghton Mifflin Company, 1931), 9, 18–19, 40, 45.

The description of Roosevelt as "all teeth and glasses" (after turning in an outlaw he had captured in the Badlands) is from Morris, *The Rise of Theodore Roosevelt.*

The description of Burroughs as "tanned" from *The Slabsides Book of John Burroughs,* p. 53. quotation regarding digging up rocks is from Renehan, *John Burroughs,* 225.

That poor construction is typical of logging roads is from Henry, *Catskill Trails,* 42–43.

Chapter 8

The quotation about the eagle's flight is from Renehan, Jr., *John Burroughs,* 201.

The description of Plattekill gorge is from Titus, *The Other Side of Time,* 22–29, and Henry, *Catskill Trails,* 48–54.

Rip Van Winkle as guardian spirit and the description of the failed venture are from Alf Evers, *In Catskill Country: Collected Essays on Mountain History, Life and Love* (Woodstock, NY: Overlook Press, 1995), 15–21.

The history of the boreal forest in the Catskills is from Michael Kudish, *The Catskill Forest: A History* (Fleischmanns, NY: Purple Mountain Press, 2000), 20–30.

Information on the balm of Gilead tree is from Evers, *The Catskills: From Wilderness to Woodstock,* 81–87.

The history of the Catskill Mountain House is available online at the Mountaintop Historical Society's Catskill Archive, www.catskillarchive. com.

Cole's approach to American landscapes is from Isaiah Smithson, "Thoreau, Thomas Cole, and Asher Durand: Composing the American Landscape," in *Thoreau's Sense of Place: Essays in American Environmental Writing,* ed. Richard J. Schneider (Iowa City: University of Iowa Press), 2000, and Lee Vedder and Elizabeth Jacks, *Thomas Cole's Creative Process* (Cedar Grove, NY: The Thomas Cole National Historic Site, undated).

Thomas Cole's comments on wildness and Eden are from his "Essay on American Scenery," *American Monthly Magazine*, January 1836.

The story of Burroughs inspiring Whitman to include the hermit thrush in his poem is from Renehan, Jr., *John Burroughs*, 82–83, and Kaplan, *Walt Whitman*, 307–8.

Chapter 9

Construction of the Schoharie Reservoir and Shandanken Tunnel in Diane Galusha, *Liquid Assets: A History of New York City's Water System* (Fleischmanns, NY: Harbor Hill Books, 1999), 155–66.

The discovery of prehistoric trees is discussed in "Oldest fossilized forest: Entire fossil forest dating back 385 million years unearthed," *ScienceDaily*, February 29, 2012.

The observation about Boyhood Rock and the eerie quiet of the ancient Gilboa forest is from Titus, *The Other Side of Time*, 9, 101.

Information on the Lansing Manor and Mine Kill State Park is available on the New York Power Authority's website, www.nypa.gov, under "Blenheim-Gilboa Visitors Center."

Chapter 10

Henry Conklin, *Through "Poverty's Vale": A Hardscrabble Boyhood in Upstate New York, 1832–1862* (Syracuse, NY: Syracuse University Press, 1974).

Visit Lisa Smith-Batchen's website, www.dreamchaserevents.com, to learn about her races, and consider having her coach you, too.

The history of Vrooman's Nose is in Vincent J. Schaefer, *Vrooman's Nose: A Study* (Fleischmanns, NY: Purple Mountain Press, 1992) and John P. D. Wilkinson, *The Schoharie Valley* (Charleston, SC: Arcadia Publishing, 2012).

The life of Joseph Brant and all quotations are from Louis Aubrey Wood, *The War Chief of the Six Nations: A Chronicle of Joseph Brant* (New York: Brook & Co., 1915), except for the statement he made before King George III, which comes from the American Indian Heritage Foundation, accessed December 16, 2015 at http://www.indians.org/welker/brant.htm.

Chapter 11

The discovery of ancient red cedar is described by TERRA (The Earth Restoration and Renewal Alliance), accessed December 16, 2015, at http://www.ancientforests.us/surveys/SchoharieEscarpment.htm.

Mohican population estimates are from a website maintained by Lee Sultzman, accessed December 16, 2015, at http://www.dickshovel.com/Mahican.html. The tribal design, "Many Trails," is visible on the website of the Mohican Nation Stockbridge-Munsee Band at www.mohican.com.

Quotations are from James Fenimore Cooper, *The Last of the Mohicans; A narrative of 1757* (Philadelphia: H. C. Carey & I. Lea, 1826), 5, 46, 95, 122.

For more information on feral pigs, see Eileen Stegemann, "Pigs Gone Wild: Feral swine threaten New York State," *New York State Conservationist*, October 2012, available on the Department of Environmental Conservation website: www.dec.ny.gov.

Chapter 12

Walt Whitman's last words to Burroughs from *The Slabsides Book of John Burroughs*, p. 86.

For more on Theodore Roosevelt's adventure in the Amazon, see Candice Millard, *The River of Doubt: Theodore Roosevelt's Darkest Journey* (New York: Anchor, 2006), and Roosevelt's own memoirs of the trip, Theodore Roosevelt, *Through the Brazilian Wilderness* (New York:

C. Scribner's Sons, 1914). Burroughs's reaction is from Kanze, *The World of John Burroughs*, p. 116. Burroughs's last words from Renehan, *John Burroughs: An American Naturalist*, p. 313.

For information on the John Burroughs Association, visit the website www.johnburroughsassociation.org. Bird-watching and other hikes and field trips are organized by the John Burroughs Natural History Society, www.jbnhs.org.